'A Flint Seasid

A GUIDE TO ST AUGUSTINE'S

*'I have a delightful plan of a flint seaside church
and everything gives way to that.'*
A.W.N.Pugin, in a letter to the Earl of Shrewsbury, c1846

Libby Horner and Gill Hunter
Foreword by Alexandra Wedgwood

THE FRIENDS OF ST AUGUSTINE'S
THE PUGIN SOCIETY

Published by The Friends of St Augustine's, Ramsgate, and The Pugin Society, Ramsgate, England

Foreword © Alexandra Wedgwood 2000

Main Text © Libby Horner and Gill Hunter 2000, Second edition 2016

Designed by Michael Pennamacoor of Abgrundrisse

Printed by Lanes (SE) Ltd, Broadstairs, Kent

All rights reserved. No part of this book may be reproduced, stored in a retrieval system, transmitted or utilised in any form or by any means, electronic, mechanical, photocopying, recording or otherwise, without the permission of the publishers.

The authors have asserted their rights to be identified as the authors of this work in accordance with the Copyright, Designs and Patents Act 1988

British Library Cataloguing in publication data

Authors: Libby Horner and Gill Hunter

Title: *A Flint Seaside Church*

ISBN: 978-1-5262-0479-0

Front Cover: detail from A.W.N.Pugin's watercolour of 1849 *A True Prospect of St Augustine's Church now erecting at Ramsgate in the Isle of Thanet* (Private collection)
Title Page: An adaptation of the Pugin coat of arms and motto by A.W.N.Pugin, containing his monogram: title page to *The True Principles of Pointed or Christian Architecture,* 1841

Contents

Acknowledgements i

Foreword: by Alexandra Wedgwood ii

1. Pugin and his world 1

2. Religion in Nineteenth Century England 9

3. The Road to Ramsgate 14

4. Guide to St Augustine's Church 16

5. Other sites of interest 49

Further reading 54

Notes 55

Acknowledgements

We are very grateful to the following for their assistance in preparing this history and guide:

Dr Margaret Belcher; Catriona Blaker; Joan Bond, Catholic Central Library; Geoff Brandwood; John Coverdale, St Augustine's Church; Professor J. Mordaunt Crook; Dr Robin Darwall-Smith, Archivist, Magdalen College, Oxford; Nick Dermott, Dip Arch, RIBA, Father Dickie, Westminster Diocesan Archive; George Downer, Former Organist, St Augustine's Church; Dr John Elliott; Rosemary Hill; Fr Marcus Holden, St Augustine's Church; Graham Horner MICE; Sarah Houle; Anna Hulbert FIIC; Michael Hunt, Ramsgate Maritime Museum; Lorna Maynard at *The Tablet*; Dr Rory O'Donnell; Rt Rev Dom Laurence O'Keeffe OSB, Abbot, St Augustine's Monastery; Rev Dom John Seddon OSB, Archivist, St Augustine's Monastery; Paul Sharrock, Thomas Ford & Partners; Dr Stanley Shepherd; staff at Southwark Diocesan Archive Office; Ann Stocker RIBA; Dr Julia Twigg; and Lady Wedgwood.

A.W.N.Pugin, early 1840s.
The only known photograph (private collection)

Foreword

More than any other nineteenth century architect, A.W.Pugin determined the style of church building throughout the world during that century. It is thanks to him that when we see pointed arches and pointed windows we automatically expect to be looking at a church. This is because he believed that Christianity and the Gothic style were inseparable, and he said and wrote so with such force that the vast majority of churches built during that major period of church building were in that style. He was a Catholic, but the Gothic Revival was taken up by all Christian denominations. Ultimately the Catholic authorities were among the least enthusiastic.

It is therefore of the greatest interest to see how he interpreted his own 'true principles' in the church which he built himself, next to his own house, lovingly and slowly at his own expense, and dedicated to his patron saint, and in which he and his family are buried. The result is a deeply felt, spiritual building, both strong and beautiful, full of the character of its designer.

I have much pleasure in recommending this book: it fills a long felt need and the Pugin Society are to be congratulated on this venture. Pugin has in recent years become far better known, and Ramsgate was the centre of his life. It will add greatly to your understanding of these buildings, their designer and his aims.

Alexandra Wedgwood

Pugin's celebrated bird's-eye view of St Augustine's and the Grange, exhibited in the Royal Academy of 1849 (private collection)

The Church grew into what it is, not in his ordinary way of estimated drawings, but fashioned by his mind as it advanced stage by stage. It is full of poetry and expression, though small, and Pugin is seen in it at his best, "because free". He told his son Edward "I am giving you the best architectural lessons I can; watch the Church, there shall not be a single 'True Principle' broken."

A.Wedgwood (ed) 'Pugin in his home', A Memoir by J.H.Powell, London, 1994, (reprinted from *Architectural History*, Vol 31: 1988)

Pugin and his world

*'one of the most remarkable men of his generation …
impetuous, prejudiced, but honest and sincere'* [1]

Pugin was an intense and determined man, driven by seemingly inexhaustible energy and by two intertwined passions, Gothic architecture and Catholicism. He yearned romantically for the Middle Ages when men built churches to the glory of God, their faith directing their endeavours; and longed for the community of souls embraced within a medieval society where devotion, charity, loyalty, hospitality, and scholarship were paramount. The Grange and St Augustine's Church represent the culmination of his theories and endeavours: his life, soul, and money went into the construction of these two buildings. Hampered, infuriated and constrained by clients' demands; by committees, which he hated; by ecclesiological differences of opinion; and by the minority status of the Catholic Church in England, Pugin felt that he had never been given the chance to realise his 'True Principles' – except in his own church where he was 'both paymaster and architect'.[2] Standing on the outskirts of Ramsgate, gazing out at the treacherous Goodwin Sands, these two buildings seem to symbolise the ostracism Pugin faced, even from his fellow Catholics.

Background
Augustus Welby Northmore Pugin was born in 1812, the only child of A.C.Pugin, a French émigré, and his wife Catherine Welby, an Evangelical Anglican. The gifted young man designed furniture for Windsor Castle at the age of fifteen, and after a brief interval creating sets for the London theatre, he married and moved to Salisbury. It was here that he became a Roman Catholic in 1835 and wrote his celebrated book *Contrasts* (1836). His reputation was consolidated by the publication of his book *The True Principles of Christian or Pointed Architecture* (1841) and by his designs for cathedrals, numerous churches, and some domestic buildings. He was the moving spirit behind the Mediæval Court at the Great Exhibition of 1851, and conceived the elaborate interiors of the Houses of Parliament. Pugin suffered a breakdown and died at the age of forty in 1852, leaving his wife Jane and the eight children of his three marriages.

A Flint Seaside Church

Theories

Pugin's graphic and architectural training came from his father, an able draughtsman and author of *Specimens of Gothic Architecture, Architectural Antiquities of Normandy, Gothic Ornaments,* and *Examples of Gothic Architecture*, the last being continued by Pugin after his father's death. Travelling with Pugin senior in search of material for these volumes trained the young boy's eye to discern the different stages of Gothic architecture, to draw more than competently, and to have the thorough understanding of styles from the twelfth to fifteenth centuries which later allowed him to recapture the essential spirit of Gothic intuitively. He wrote to his friend, the Rev John Rouse Bloxam (1807–91), fellow of Magdalen College, Oxford, 'I seek *antiquity* not *novelty*. I strive to *revive* not *invent*.'[3]

Pugin is often regarded as the archetypal Goth, largely because he was articulate, a self-publicist and polemicist. No one could write like him, *and* produce designs for metalwork, stained glass and furniture; and no one had his hypermanic zeal. Pugin himself thought that his writings, rather than his buildings, 'have revolutionised the taste of England'[4] and both Hermann Muthesius and Sir Nikolaus Pevsner – to mention two of many – recognised his seminal role with respect to the evolution of nineteenth and twentieth-century architectural and design theories.

In *The True Principles of Christian or Pointed Architecture* Pugin closed with an exhortation to fellow architects and artists to 'Let then the Beautiful and the True be our watchword for future exertions in the overthrow of modern paltry taste and paganism, and the revival of Catholic art and dignity'.[5] He felt that buildings pleased because of their beauty, instructed by their symbolism, and, essentially, provided shelter. A plan would be devised which accommodated the requirements of the occupants, and from this the building would develop, in an organic manner, the outer shape of the building expressing its form and function. In Pugin's words 'the external and internal appearance of an edifice should be illustrative of, and in accordance with, the purpose for which it is destined';[6] 'the architecture and arrangement [of buildings] have originated in their wants and purpose'.[7] He was advocating structural integrity; what is now known as 'functionalism'.

Pugin said, 'building for the sake of uniformity never entered into the ideas of the ancient designers',[8] and 'the idea of everything being exactly alike on both sides, has created an unreal style of building'.[9] He wanted to escape the 'two and two system of modern building',[10] exemplified by the Neo-Classical style of the day, and claimed that asymmetry was 'the true spirit of pointed design, and until the present regular system of building both sides of a church exactly alike can be broken up, no real good can be expected'.[11]

Pugin and his World

Pugin himself championed the vernacular, considering that Gothic architecture had developed naturally from the English soil and local materials. He hoped to emulate 'the ancient builders [who adapted] their edifices to localities, [so] that they seemed as if they formed a portion of nature itself ... growing from the sites in which they are placed'.[12]

These principles express the rational side of Pugin's character, but he was also a Romantic. He believed that morality and art were indivisible in the Middle Ages, and that good art and architecture were produced by men whose souls were pure, a view also found in the work of Pugin's contemporaries Cobbett (1763–1835), Carlyle (1795–1881), Kenelm Digby (1800–80) and J.S.Mill (1806–73). Pugin used his theory to damn the Renaissance as a period of 'pagan art' produced by a society which had turned its back on true Christian values. His aesthetic and social enthusiasm drove him to promote the re-establishment of Gothic which, to him, perfectly evoked the pre-Reformation Catholic Church: 'the faith, the zeal, and above all, the unity, of our ancestors, [which] enabled them to conceive and raise those wonderful fabrics'.[13]

Functionalism, organic and vernacular architecture, expressionism – these are all twentieth-century words, but not wholly out of place when considering Pugin's principles, because, stripped of their Gothicism, his rules are Spartan, basic and still pertinent today.

Pugin was a master of linear, two-dimensional pattern. He claimed that designers in the middle ages worked directly from nature, neither copying from previous work nor inventing, but creating stylised images inspired by the original. 'The foliage is *natural*, and it is the *adaptation* and *disposition* of it which stamps the style'.[14] Pugin's own work in the design of wallpaper, carpets, curtains, stained glass and tiles reflected these views, and laid the foundations for the artistic theories and designs of such men as William Morris (1834–96) and Christopher Dresser (1834–1904). The decorative motifs in the church, whether in stained glass or tiling, are successfully two-dimensional; red and yellow predominating, the colours of Pugin's shield.

Scholarship

Undoubtedly, Pugin's precocious scholarship derived from the influence of his father. The elder Pugin had a considerable collection of antiquities and an extensive library, much of which was sold in 1833 after his death; the catalogue of the four-day sale of his books, prints, drawings and casts giving an idea of its extent and quality. The young Pugin started building up his own collection at an early age, travelling home from Christchurch in 1825 with 'two large chests full of antiquities'.[15]

A Flint Seaside Church

According to Benjamin Ferrey (1808–1880), a pupil of A.C.Pugin, the son was collecting books and manuscripts, as well as prints and pictures, by the time he was residing at St Marie's, the house he designed for himself near Salisbury, in 1835. This is corroborated by a watercolour view of the interior of St Marie's, showing the well-stocked shelves of Pugin's library. John Hardman Powell, Pugin's son-in-law and only pupil, describes Pugin's library at Ramsgate, the shelves holding his books of reference 'all handy'. Pugin was obviously proud of his collection, entreating Bloxam, 'I beg of you to use my Library as you would your own'.[16]

After his death, S. Leigh Sotheby and John Wilkinson of London conducted a sale of Pugin's books in January 1853, all six hundred and forty-five lots raising £1,083 12s 6d. Further sales of pictures and objets d'art by Sotheby's in 1853 scattered most of Pugin's acquisitions, some items being purchased by the British Museum and the Museum of Ornamental Art at Marlborough House (now part of the collections of the Victoria and Albert Museum).

The most convincing evidence of Pugin's ecclesiastical and architectural erudition is provided by his own publications. *Contrasts* reflects his knowledge of fifteenth, sixteenth and seventeenth-century books, particularly those containing woodcut illustrations. Pugin was also familiar with the works of his friend, Kenelm Digby, such as *The Broad Stone of Honour*, and *Mores Catholici*, both of which extolled the medieval way of life. In his *True Principles*, Pugin argued that 'the smallest detail should have a meaning or serve a purpose', and his extensive scholarship would have rendered him one of the few who appreciated the symbolism of such minutiae. Pugin's familiarity with details of ancient building construction, tiles, textiles and metalwork derived not only from observation of them *in situ* and in museums on his journeys to France, Germany, Italy, Switzerland and the Low Countries, but also from his own collection. He provided examples to inspire his workmen, explaining that, 'they will be very useful for no drawing can give these things'.[17] His cartoon room in the courtyard of The Grange, for instance, contained 'fine carvings and casts'[18] according to Powell, who described one carved oak newel post which Pugin had snatched out of a fire, 'the charred parts show what a narrow escape it had.'[19]

Charity

Charitable acts were of the greatest importance to Pugin, and he illustrated what he considered to be essential communal buildings, schools, town halls, even inns and public water pumps in his book *Contrasts*. In the second edition, published in 1841, he drew particular attention to the secular workhouses of the nineteenth century, comparing them with the benefits of the residences for the poor provided by the medieval Church. Pugin was anxious to provide such facilities at Ramsgate, purchasing, in 1849, land behind St Augustine's where there would be 'room for

Pugin and his World

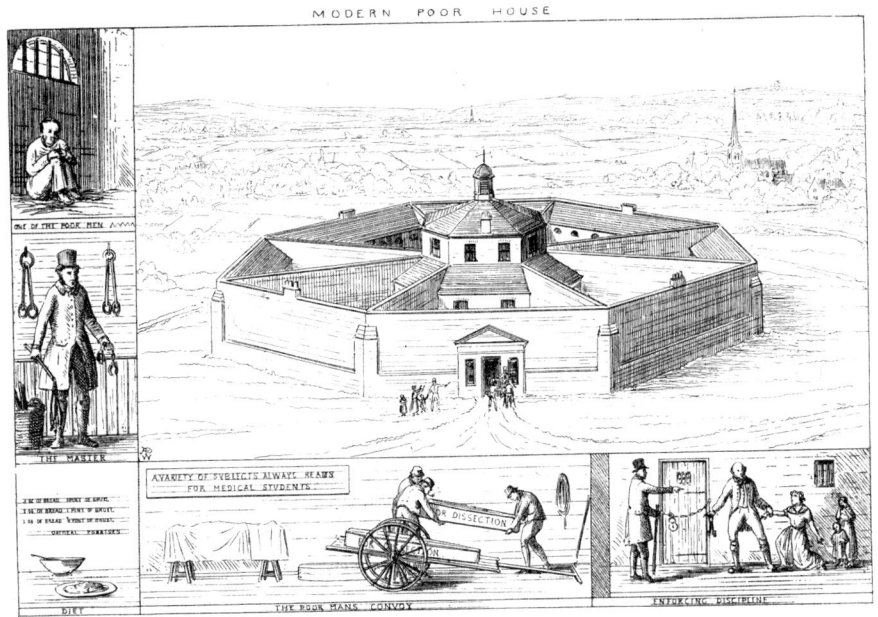

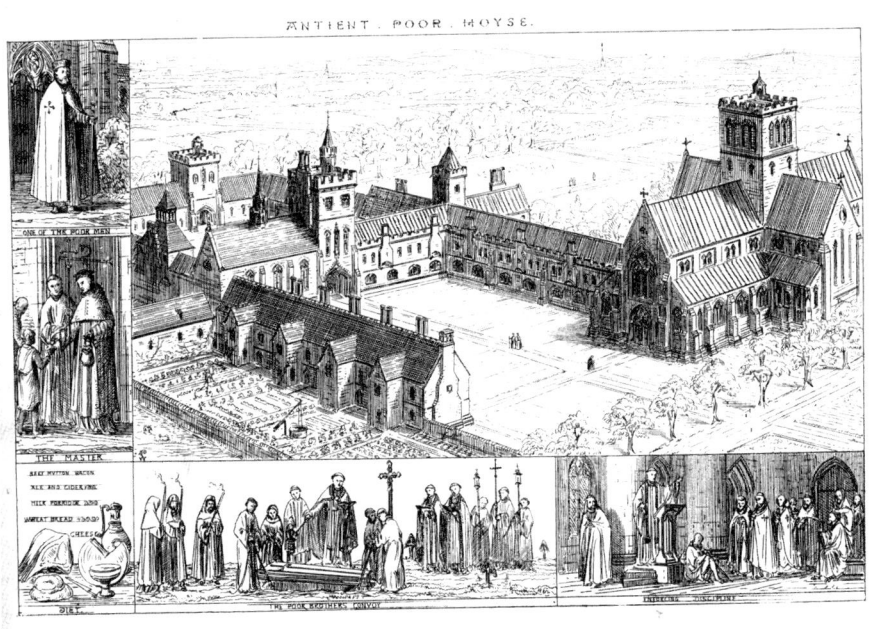

1. The treatment of the poor in the nineteenth century and in medieval times: Pugin's telling indictment of contemporary society in the second edition (1841) of *Contrasts*

A Flint Seaside Church

schools, house for Christian brothers, sisters of mercy, girls' school, alms-house and presbytery etc.'[20]

Pugin was especially concerned for the welfare of mariners, many of whom were brought ashore injured when their vessels foundered on the Goodwins, as well as providing a Catholic burial for those who perished. He believed he 'must have a hospital here – about six beds would do, but it is dreadful to see these poor people from disabled and wrecked ships literally perished with want and cold'.[21] On 25 September 1852, *The Builder* reminded readers how Pugin had taken home and nursed Spanish sailors sick with fever. It is believed that Pugin rented two houses in King Street, Ramsgate, and paid for staff to attend sick seamen there.

Besides the physical necessities of mariners, Pugin was, of course, anxious to minister to their spiritual needs. James Jauch, the priest of St Boniface's (the chapel for the German Catholics in London), reported in *The Tablet* on 27 December 1845 that on walking round Ramsgate harbour and discovering 170 German emigrants en route to the United States, Pugin, his host, arranged that they should attend Mass at his house the following day. His private chapel being far too small to accommodate such a throng, Pugin arranged his studio [in all probability the cartoon room] with a temporary altar, cross and candles, so that Jauch could celebrate Mass. As soon as the present sacristy of St Augustine's was completed and in use as a chapel, Pugin had notices of the times of services printed in six languages and 'distributed by a Catholic shipping agent belonging to the port to all foreign vessels on their arrival.'[22] Once services could be held in St Augustine's Church, this room was put to use as a school for the education of local Catholic children. However, this proved to be an unsuccessful venture; the boys were unruly and, having discovered that 'the little beasts' had stolen his coal, Pugin closed it down.[23]

Although in his correspondence Pugin expressed his discomfort at keeping servants, he retained an old labourer as a gardener, because the man had

2. Pugin's drawing of the *Caroline*: letter to John Hardman, 1849

Pugin and his World

'splintered an Eye chopping wood for the house, and was a pensioner with his wife until death.'[24] Pugin's charity was all-embracing: he believed that life was too short for 'chasing up only deserving cases',[25] even though he realised he was sometimes duped. Powell recounts that 'he literally gave away his boots more than once and walked home without,'[26] and Trappes-Lomax recorded that Pugin kept a chest of clothes in the entrance hall of The Grange, to be distributed amongst the needy.[27]

Pugin was modest about his charity, only mentioning it when trying to appease the inhabitants of Ramsgate at the height of the 'Papal Aggression' disturbances in 1850. He pointed out in his billposter that:

> I have endeavoured to serve God in peace, and live in charity with all. I have contributed, as far as my limited means would permit, in works of general usefulness and indiscriminate charity ... I have for many years shared the fatted ox with people, many of whose religious principles are the very antipodes of my own; but I am willing to believe them sincere in what they profess, and their poverty is a sufficient claim to their treatment as brethren.[28]

Sailing

Ferrey records that Pugin bought his first boat in the late 1820s, much to his parents' regret. Pugin presumably kept it on the Thames, for his diary for May 1831 records, 'Started from Westminster Bridge in my own boat, Elizabeth' and 'Left Gravesend 6 am ... reached Westminster at 6 o'clock pm.'[29] As he was known to continue drawing and sketching during such trips, it must be assumed that he did not sail the boat himself. However, Pugin had a sailor's preoccupation with the weather, remarking that, 'I would not leave the pier in a heavy gale of wind for the Pope. It is the only comfort I have in the world, the only thing that relieves my mind ... if the Pope Emperor and all the crowned and mitred heads in Europe wanted anything done in SSW gales they would not get it. It is my only ressource.'[30]

Pugin noted in his diary on 21 February 1849, 'Bought the lugger Caroline with Mr Luck for £70'.[31] A Bill of Sale dated 7 March 1849 shows that Pugin and his friend Alfred Luck (1807/8–64), a wealthy local resident, held 27/64ths each, with William Miller, one of the previous owners, retaining 10/64ths.[32] The *Caroline* was built at Deal in 1824, and registered at Sandwich in May of that year. Later registration, on 26 January 1841, describes her as a three masted lugger, just over forty feet long and thirteen feet wide, clench built, with square stern and running bowsprit.

The Goodwin Sands is a large bank of shifting sands lying about six miles east of the Kent coast. It forms the eastern shelter of an anchorage known as the Downs, which is protected on the west by the North and South Forelands. This

A Flint Seaside Church

was always a busy anchorage, where vessels entering the Thames picked up their pilot, and those leaving it dropped theirs. Sometimes dozens of ships would be at anchor there, waiting for a fair wind to enter the Thames or to sail down-Channel. Luggers were employed retrieving and supplying replacement gear to damaged ships (hovelling), ferrying personnel and stores between ship and shore (foying), as well as saving lives and cargoes from wrecked ships, and possibly even smuggling.[33] Many ships foundered on the treacherous Goodwins, and from the tower of his house Pugin would have been one of the first to observe their fate. At times he made considerable sums from salvage operations, as he informed Crace, '£160 [awarded] to my boat for services rendered during the last gale … a good job for me',[34] and 'my boat was first at the wreck of the Belgian schooner bound for Rio … They brought off silks and laces, insured for between 1 and 2 thousand pounds … it will be the best hoard of the Season and in May!!!!'[35]

Pugin travelled regularly to Europe, where he bought antiquities of all kinds, both secular and ecclesiastical. Ferrey described these 'excursions as subservient to the object of forming a museum, which later in his life afforded him the greatest pleasure'.[36] Pugin also supplied items, either directly or through dealers, to several of his projects. Pugin may well have been encouraged by the duty on antiquities, £1 per square foot on paintings and 1/- per pound weight on manuscripts, to land his continental purchases below St Augustine's, and carry them up to his home through tunnels in the cliffs. Such activities are intimated in a teasing remark about 'smuggling over antiquities for sale',[37] although Pugin took pains to maintain a close relationship with the deputy Harbour Master, Captain Shaw, who visited The Grange each week to talk 'about sea affairs'.[38]

On 2nd of July 1849, Luck sold his share in the *Caroline* to Pugin, but on 13th February 1852 a bill of sale records that she was sold to George Leffin, a mariner of Ramsgate, prompted, presumably, by Pugin's failing health.

3. Detail from an engraving of a painting of the Goodwin Sands by Clarkson Stanfield RA, Pugin's friend, who often stayed at The Grange

Religion in Nineteenth Century England

Roman Catholicism

The Roman Catholic faith had been kept alive in England since the Reformation by the few old aristocratic recusant families. Their meditative and emotionally restrained style of worship had been promoted by Bishop Richard Challoner (1691–1781) in his book, *Garden of the Soul, A Manual of Spiritual Exercises and Instructions for Christians who (living in the world) aspire to Devotion*, which by 1750 had become the most influential spiritual work for English Catholics. This sober and gentle treatise advocated charity, referring to the faithful as Christians, not Catholics. With the passing of the Roman Catholic Relief Acts of 1778 and 1791, and by avoiding controversy and exclusivity, the numbers of practising Catholics had gradually increased, with the authorities turning a blind eye to the publication of Catholic books and provision of limited education.

The most notable of Pugin's Catholic patrons was the Earl of Shrewsbury. A scion of one of the leading Catholic families, John Talbot (1791–1852), succeeded his uncle to become 16th Earl of Shrewsbury and Waterford in June 1827. In August 1837 Pugin visited him at his seat, Alton Towers, having been recommended by Shrewsbury's private chaplain, Dr Daniel Rock (1799–1871), who wrote to congratulate Pugin on the publication of *Designs for Gold & Silversmiths* (1836). Pugin was to assist Shrewsbury in completing the alterations begun at the Towers by the 15th Earl, and, with the encouragement of Shrewsbury's friend, Ambrose Phillipps de Lisle, he designed the Hospital of St John the Baptist at Alton. Besides funding this undertaking, Shrewsbury was also responsible for the Church of St Mary, Uttoxeter (1838–39) and the Church of St Giles, Cheadle (1841–46), as well as donations to numerous other building projects designed by Pugin. Through Shrewsbury's influence, Pugin was appointed Professor of Ecclesiastical Architecture at St Mary's College, Oscott, his lectures there forming the basis of *True Principles*.

Ambrose Phillipps (1809–78), who later took the name de Lisle, also proved an important Catholic patron. Despite his family's opposition to his conversion to Catholicism at the age of fifteen, Phillipps inherited extensive estates in Leicestershire in 1862. Phillipps purchased land in Charnwood Forest, Leicestershire, and in 1840, appointed Pugin architect of Mount St Bernard's

A Flint Seaside Church

Monastery for the Cistercian Order, later to become the first canonical abbey to be built in England since the Reformation. Realising the significance of the project, Pugin refused to accept a fee for his work.

The enormous increase in the Catholic population of England and Wales from approximately eighty thousand in 1770 to approximately three-quarters of a million in 1850,[39] was due in part to the 1846–49 Famine in Ireland. Vast numbers of Irish immigrants settled in the manufacturing towns, particularly in the north and west of England. The militant style of many Protestant evangelical sects in the large conurbations was adopted by the Catholic clergy in the battle for souls. Priests and missionary religious orders worked tirelessly in appalling conditions, where cholera and typhus were rife, to establish support from cradle to grave. The rather lax Irish Catholicism, imbued with folk belief, and the discreet worship of the recusant Catholics, was replaced by devotional fervour expressed through public devotions and ceremonies, including the Benediction of the Blessed Sacrament, and the use of the Rosary. These practices, and the veneration of the Blessed Virgin Mary and later of the Sacred Heart, often passionately adopted by converts, reflected the sense of a religious revival.

With his attitude to charity and emphasis on medieval English vestments and plainchant, Pugin appears to have advocated what he called an 'English' Catholicism. He pointed out that:

> our ancestors were not Roman Catholics they were English catholics. Of course in communion with Rome. We have had an English Church from the days of the Blessed Austin. … Never acknowledge a Roman Catholic. We are of the old school of our Edwards, Anselms, Thomas's, Englishmen to the back bone.[40]

When Pugin took up residence in St Lawrence, Ramsgate in 1833, the only Catholic place of worship in Thanet was an inconspicuous chapel which had been built in Prospect Place, Margate in 1804. In 1820, the incumbent was Father Thomas Costigan (1788–1860), an Irish priest, who travelled as far afield as Rye, Romney, Hythe, Dover and Deal to serve the scattered Catholic community in eastern Kent. From the end of 1846, Catholic visitors to Ramsgate, as well as sailors, could hear Mass at St Augustine's, sparing them the walk along the windswept coast to Margate. By 1852 there was a resident priest in Ramsgate, whilst the beginning of a vigorous Catholic mission to Kent was marked by the arrival in the town of the Benedictine monk, Father Wilfrid Alcock, in 1856.

For many years English Catholics had petitioned Rome for their own hierarchy so that they would have greater control of their own affairs. This was eventually granted in 1850, Pope Pius IX appointing Nicholas Wiseman, previously his Vicar-Apostolic of London, as Cardinal and Archbishop of Westminster. The tone of Wiseman's first pastoral letter announcing his appointment roused a fury of anti-

Papism, with *The Times* raging against the so-called 'Papal Aggression'. In Ramsgate, Pugin suffered: 'walls and gates are chalked with insults too gross and obscene to commit to paper'.[41] Pugin responded forcefully with a pamphlet, *An Address to the People of Ramsgate*, in which he pointed out that this was an 'attack on the very liberties of the country, which, at the same time, you pretend to protect.'[42]

With the introduction of the new centralised hierarchy of Roman educated clergy, who established a disciplined and conservative administration, the influence of the old Catholic gentry was eroded. Unfortunately for Pugin, this was accompanied by the claim that Classical, rather than Gothic, architecture best expressed the Roman rite. John Henry Newman wrote:

> Mr. Pugin is a man of genius; I have the greatest admiration for his talents, and willingly acknowledge that Catholics owe him a great debt for what he has done in the revival of Gothic architecture among us ... But he has the great fault of a man of genius, as well as the merit. He is intolerant, and if I might use a strong word, a bigot. He sees nothing good in any school of Christian art except that of which he is himself so great an ornament. The canons of Gothic architecture are to him points of faith, and everyone is a heretic who would venture to question them.[43]

The Church of England: (1) The Oxford Movement

The Oxford Movement aimed to restore the High Church tradition of the Church of England and reassert its catholic inheritance. In part a reaction to the economic and social changes of industrialisation, it found parallel expression in the Romantic Movement and its espousal of the gothic. The 'expressions of a romantic age ... entered Christian devotion'[44] with the publication in 1827 of *The Christian Year*, a book of verses for each Sunday, by John Keble (1792–1866), a fellow of Oriel College, Oxford. In 1828, John Henry Newman (1801–90), also a fellow of Oriel, became vicar of the University Church of St Mary the Virgin. At this time Newman saw liberalism, expressed by the Catholic Emancipation Act of 1829 which finally allowed Roman Catholics to sit in Parliament and to hold most civil and military offices, as a spiritual and moral evil. Newman, Keble and others formed an association to defend the established Church of Ireland, which the government was reorganising. A policy of amalgamation which effectively abolished eight Irish bishoprics and two archbishoprics provoked Keble to preach a sermon in the University Church on 14 July 1833, in which he condemned it as an act of 'national apostasy'. This is commonly regarded as the beginning of the Oxford Movement.

In order to encourage greater spirituality, discipline and worship within the Church of England, Keble and Newman decided to circulate tracts advocating apostolic succession, daily prayer, regular communion, and the upholding of the *Book of Common Prayer*. In 1840 Pugin began corresponding with Newman's curate, Bloxam, to whom he wrote, 'it does me good to see you. I never meet with so much sympathy for any one else even the revival men are for the most part tinctured with Protestantism and Paganism.'[45] Pugin endorsed the movement enthusiastically, explaining that:

> when we see the glorious works which are daily put forth by the Oxford men can we doubt that God has great things in store for us. All this will be brought about by the Anglicans and I think it is our bounden duty to assist them and advise in every way.[46]

Newman increasingly came to see the Church of England as a political creation, manipulated by Parliament, particularly when, in 1840, the Archbishop of Canterbury presented a petition to the House of Lords to change the wording of the Thirty Nine Articles, by which, in 1576, the doctrine of the church had been defined. Newman and others at Oxford opposed any alteration of the Articles by anyone outside the Church, and especially objected to interference by a Parliament which included Irish Catholic members. In *Tract XC*, published on 27 February 1841, Newman examined the catholicity of the Articles: looking at the wording of the Articles in almost legal terms he found them no barrier to Catholic faith. Naturally, this was construed as Roman Catholic and seen as dangerous because it destroyed the differences between the Church of England and the Church of Rome. Pressure was put on the Bishop of Oxford to prevent the publication of further tracts and Newman retired to Littlemore, where he came to realise that only the Church of Rome could withstand the forces of liberalism. He resigned his living of the University Church in 1843 and finally joined the Roman Catholic Church in 1845.

(2) Ecclesiology

The spirit of Romanticism provoked a widespread interest in archaeology and antiquarianism, and there had been a growing interest in Gothic architecture from the eighteenth century. It was Pugin, however, who argued in *Contrasts* that only if the beliefs of the Middle Ages were revived could the architecture of that period be recreated. At Trinity College, Cambridge, John Mason Neale (1818–66), Benjamin Webb (1819–85) and others founded the Cambridge Camden Society (later to be known as the Ecclesiological Society) in May 1839 to 'promote the study of Ecclesiastical Architecture and Antiquities and the restoration of mutilated Architectural remains'.[47] Although the society commissioned Pugin to design their seal, his Catholicism barred him from membership.[48]

Religion in Nineteenth Century England

The society was controlled forcibly by its committee, who also formed the editorial board of its mouthpiece, the *Ecclesiologist*, first published in November 1841. Through this publication's dogmatic insistence on construction according to *True Principles*, including the specific, symbolic significance of every detail, Pugin's influence on the buildings of the Church of England was profound. Pugin praised the society's pamphlets, *A Few Words to Church Builders* and *A Few Words to Church Wardens*:

> They do not treat the ecclesiastical antiquities of this country as mere architectural curiosities; or pointed architecture as a matter of arbitrary taste … but they set forth the construction and decoration of the temples dedicated to God in the true light, as matters of Catholic tradition, and propose the ancient Catholic structures as the only models for imitation.[49]

However, by 1846 Pugin's Catholicism had become an embarrassment to the society. The *Ecclesiologist* distanced itself from him with a bitter attack, claiming that 'Mr. Pugin, clever and enthusiastic as he is, has not answered the expectations which were formed of him; he has not realised that highest standard of Christian art which we expected from him; … while all about him were in breathless progress.'[50] Only after Pugin's death was this view modified somewhat in his obituary in the same journal.

Pugin's Influence

Pugin's Catholicism deterred major patronage from the Church of England: the only complete new Anglican church built to his design is St Lawrence, Tubney (1844), a work executed through the patronage of Bloxam. Despite Pugin's optimism, the Oxford Movement did not steer the Church of England back into the Catholic fold; nor did the revival of Roman Catholicism in England result in the adoption of the Gothic style by the new hierarchy. The success of Pugin's principles, promulgated by the *Ecclesiologist*, can, however, be judged by their profound impact on the building of new churches and the restoration of ancient ones for the Church of England, not only in Britain but also in her growing Empire.

3 The Road to Ramsgate

Pugin delighted in buildings grouped in the medieval way. Wherever he built a church, a presbytery and school are generally to be found, a first step towards the ideal. Shrewsbury commissioned the Hospital of St John the Baptist, Alton, the first large-scale community Pugin designed. The plans were drawn up in 1839, and construction took place between 1840–52, with later additions by his son Edward Pugin. The buildings are, in the monastic tradition, grouped round three sides of a quadrangle, and the apparently haphazard way in which the elements appear to the eye would lead one to imagine the development had taken place over centuries. At Mount St Bernard's Abbey, despite the ascetic strictures of Cistercian planning, and probable shortage of funds, which severely limited architectural scope, Pugin produced a gloriously romantic conglomeration. This captured the imagination of Burne-Jones who declared 'more and more my heart is pining for that monastery in Charnwood Forest ... I saw it when I was little and have hankered for it ever since'.[51]

From these projects there is a natural progression to Pugin's own Catholic community at Ramsgate. What exactly drew him to this increasingly popular middle-class seaside resort with its rail services to London and ferry services to France and Flanders? There were probably three over-riding reasons, the first being the religious connection with his patron saint, Augustine of Canterbury, who landed at Ebbsfleet in 597, bringing Christianity to southern England. Pugin's own mission, to re-ignite Catholicism, was merely a part of the continuing history of the area, symbolised by the stained glass window in The Grange showing the Isle of Thanet with the original religious settlements, to which he was prepared to add another. The task proved somewhat problematic because 'it is a most difficult place to work in lying so very much out of the way', explained Pugin, adding that 'the execution of gothic work is attended with ... vexation and trouble both to Employers and builders and it is quite a relief to my mind when the job is satisfactorily completed'.[52]

Secondly, Pugin had escaped to Ramsgate and the kindly presence of his maiden aunt, Selina Welby, whenever disaster struck. He sought solace there after the death of his first wife, and returned again after the death of his parents. The third reason was undoubtedly the lure of the turbulent grey sea. By 1843 building lots were selling fast in Ramsgate, and a site on the edge of town, overlooking Pegwell Bay and cornfields, would have appealed to Pugin, even if he was not deluded by the sale details penned by Geo. M.Hinds, architect and surveyor, who drew attention to the 'highly picturesque' scenery and the 'pure soft water from the Ramsgate Water Works' which could be 'easily supplied'.[53]

In 1852 *The Builder* stated that St Augustine's had been built 'for the benefit of the faithful residing in Ramsgate, and of the foreign seamen using the harbour',[54] and Pugin himself observed that there were 'upwards of 300 catholic sailors here for the most part *fishermen*'.[55] In 1848 *The Tablet* recorded that the many Catholic visitors and Clergy 'who resort to the sea to recruit their health' were using the church, and that 'every morning during the past week six masses have been celebrated in the two chapels, and on Sunday last the first High Mass in the whole of Thanet since the Reformation, was sung by the Very Rev Dr Weedall ... the sermon was preached by the Rev W.Hunt, of the Spanish Chapel'.[56]

It is clear that, although St Augustine's was Pugin's own undertaking, he intended from the start to cede it, free from any encumbrance, to the church, telling Bishop Thomas Griffiths (1791–1847), Vicar-Apostolic of the London District from 1836, that he required 'no assistance whatever and all I beg of your Lordship is your benediction'.[57] He also intended 'to be able to accomplish the endowment by an insurance on my life',[58] and his diary entry for 10 November 1848 reads 'insured my life for 2,000 in the Victoria'.[59] He even wrote to Hardman stating that he 'should like St Augustine's mark to be engraved on all the things as they will be inserted in an inventory attached to the deed of gift'.[60] A Deed of Gift was finally drawn up on 19 November 1846. Although the church was £2,000 in debt at the time of Pugin's death, his family honoured his commitment by paying off debts, and his builder George Myers graciously waived payment for the font (£225), screen (£92 15s 5d) and tabernacle (£110). The Bishop of Southwark's pastoral letter dated 2 October 1853 expressed the hope that the faithful would respect the founder's memory by helping to clear the debts outstanding at his death.

The Catholic Directory and Ecclesiastical Calendar for the Year 1852 recorded the Rev O.Chevalier as resident priest at St Augustine's, and noted the following services:

> RAMSGATE, St Augustine's, Rev. O. Chevalier. On Sunds. High Mass at 10 $^{1/2}$, and Serm. V. at 3, with Benedic. And Instruc. Ros. And Catech. At 6. On H.Ds. High Mass at 10 $^{1/2}$, V. at 6, with Benedic. On W.Ds. Mass at 8 $^{1/2}$. On Thurs. Benedic. At 6. On Sat. Confess. From 4 P.M.

4 Guide to St Augustine's Church

NOTE: St Augustine's and The Grange are both designated Grade I listed buildings. Pugin originally named his house St Augustine's, but it is referred to here by its later name of The Grange. The latter has now been fully restored by the Landmark Trust.

Pugin's Colleagues

Pugin's Mediæval Court at the Great Exhibition of 1851 provided a showcase for exhibits by John Gregory Crace, John Hardman, Herbert Minton and George Myers. These were the individuals with whom Pugin executed all his major commissions: men who could interpret his rough sketches and produce work to his high standards.

John Gregory Crace (1809–89) supervised the decoration of the Mediæval Court. Crace's family firm manufactured wallpaper, furniture and stained glass, and designed complete furnishing schemes, for the luxury end of the market.

John Hardman (1812–67) was a partner in his Catholic family's button-making business until his meeting with Pugin; their close friendship stimulated him to begin producing ecclesiastical ornaments. Besides decorative metalwork, Hardman also produced stained glass for Pugin from 1845, working to designs produced in the cartoon room in Ramsgate and sent up to Birmingham. His nephew, John Hardman Powell, who married Pugin's eldest daughter, Anne, became the firm's chief stained glass designer after Pugin's death.

Herbert Minton (1793–1858) had experimented for years with the production of encaustic tiles, with encouragement from Pugin, who had a collection of medieval examples. Having bought the patent rights and moulds from Samuel Wright of Stoke-on-Trent, who had registered the patent in 1830, Minton was manufacturing encaustic tiles in commercial quantities by 1836. The tiles were produced by inlaying a pattern of different coloured clay(s), which bonded to the background in the firing process, forming an indelible design.

George Myers(1803–75), a mason and builder of Hull, was the main contractor for most of Pugin's buildings, because, as Pugin said, 'he knows the sort of work I must have and his Boys are the best carvers in the country'.[61] Powell described him as 'a man after Pugin's heart, full of energy ... [who] had a profound respect for the genius of Pugin, following his instructions with fidelity.'[62]

The understanding and assistance of these co-workers was essential to the building of St Augustine's: they recognised Pugin's requirements, appreciated his financial difficulties and acknowledged his pre-eminence in the revival of Gothic design.

Intentions and Costs

Powell described St Augustine's as 'a thorough Thanet Church, a natural growth of the locality',[63] built, where possible, of traditional, local materials, and based on the thirteenth and fourteenth-century Kentish churches. Pugin was undoubtedly familiar with the local churches and his diaries record those he visited in the summer of 1849, Ash, Birchington, Chartham, Chilham, Eastry, Eastwell, Herne, Littlebourne, Monkton, Reculver, St Nicholas-at-Wade, Sandwich, Sturry, Wickhambreaux, Wingham and Wye.

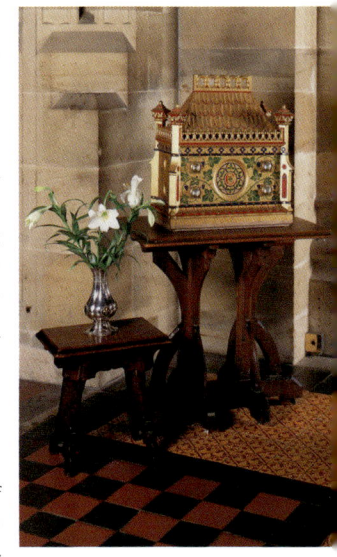

4. Pugin altar vase, stool, reliquary and table

One delightfully medieval aspect of the construction, according to Powell, was that Pugin drew one ground plan, and nothing more. The church developed as and when money became available, 'fashioned by his mind as it advanced stage by stage'.[64] In this context it is interesting to consider the sketch sent to Bishop Griffiths in October 1844, which shows the church, priest's house and cloister almost as built, the major differences being the position of the south porch, the fenestration in the tower, the lack of steeple, lack of sacristy and bell turret, and the west cloister which was added after Pugin's death. Another sketch plan sent to Bloxam in September 1845 shows a complete cloister, central tower, a lady chapel shorter than the chancel, a four-bay nave, and

5. Pugin's sketch of his proposed church: letter to Bishop Griffiths, 1844

A Flint Seaside Church

the south porch at the baptistry end of the south aisle. Creating the 'whole of the drawings on a sheet of cartridge paper'[65] with only a stump of pencil and a carpenter's rule, was Pugin's usual working method, facilitated by the fact that he could rely on his colleagues to translate and carry out his intentions instinctively and intuitively. In true medieval fashion, Pugin allowed individuals a certain freedom of expression.

Pugin was deeply frustrated by the slow progress of his church. Seven years in the making (1845–52), it was not complete at his death. This delay was linked to Pugin's finances, which, in his last years, became less stable due to the lack of church commissions and his own recurring illnesses. Having been bankrupt early in his working career, he had a terror of repeating this mistake, and the detailed accounts he kept as a result are highly illuminating.

His account book, now in the Victoria and Albert Museum[66], shows that between September 1844 and February 1852 Pugin spent a total of £14,813 14s 9 1/2d on his church. Of this, £427 was paid to Hardman for metalwork and some stained glass, and £9,341 to Myers. The latter presented a single bill for £2,200 in 1846, one bill for £966 in 1847, two bills amounting to £1,986 in 1848, and six bills totalling £3,684 in 1849. The remaining £504 was spread over the following three years. After 1850 it appears from the accounts that Pugin paid the labourers' wages on a weekly basis. The account book does not include payments to Crace or Minton, and Hardman appears to have invoiced separately for the remainder of the stained glass, the archives indicating a further outlay of £802 of which, however, about £500 was paid for by gifts.[67] It seems that the church, including all fitments, furniture, plate, vestments and books, cost approximately £20,000.

Materials

St Augustine's church is built on a chalk cliff and the ground slopes down quite steeply from north to south, requiring several floor levels within the cloisters. The exterior is faced with flint, a local material, which, when cut (knapped), reveals a silica core, particularly resistant to weathering. Many thirteenth and fourteenth-century Kentish churches were constructed of flint, usually rough, sometimes knapped, put together with mortar on a rubble core. On buildings further inland, there is typically more mortar exposed but at St Augustine's, the flints are carefully placed and galletted (with small chips of flint set into the joints), to produce a solid, black, glittering, erosion-resistant façade.

Although durable, flint is deficient in longitudinal and transverse strength, and was traditionally laid in sections between brick or stone bands, with similar dressings round windows, doors and quoins. Pugin probably appreciated the decorative quality of this building technique, but instead of the wide bands one finds on the lower stage of the tower at St Martin's, Herne for instance, Pugin used

St Augustine's Church

fine sections of sandstone, the yellow tone softening the otherwise stark exterior. No local stone being available, Pugin chose sandstone from quarries near Whitby, Yorkshire, because of its durability, its links to St Hilda's Abbey perched on a similarly exposed site and because the stone was relatively cheap, apparently being brought south as ballast. The first stage of the complex, the narrow two-storey east cloister and sacristy, was built without banding.

Building in such an exposed position on the cliffs overlooking Pegwell Bay, to a design which, unusually for Pugin, did not include buttresses, but desiring something '*very solid*',[68] he used brick rather than the more conventional rubble core. Glimpses of the buff Medway stock bricks can be seen in the south porch and above the cross-beams, looking eastward towards the tower, in the nave. The meticulous accounts for the church reveal that at least £881 was spent on brick, which, at a cost of 38s/1000, would imply more than 463,000 bricks.

Although the interior walls of most old Kentish churches were plastered, Pugin wanted the very best for his church. Consequently the entire interior, walls, pillars, and window reveals, is faced with random coursed, plain jointed Whitby ashlar, the current bedding of the sandstone producing warm shades of yellow, buff and grey. Pugin used these subtle colour variations to advantage and, to ensure the best workmanship, employed twenty Scottish stonemasons.[69] An ardent advocate of Gregorian hymns, Pugin reported in delight to Lord Shrewsbury that 'the sound of chanting is quite like that of our old cathedrals as it is all stone'.[70] Rather than employ the traditional Kentish red roof tiles found on most local churches, Pugin preferred a toning grey colour, and, again unusually for Kent, opted for alternate bands of decorative and plain tiles made in Staffordshire.

Stained Glass

Stained glass played an important part in all Pugin's churches, and illustrates his desire to return to the traditional medieval craft, where the design is defined by the leadwork enclosing pieces of coloured glass, rather than sheets of painted glass. Dissatisfied with the manufacturers Warrington (1786–1869), Willement (1786–1871) and Wailes (1808–81), Pugin persuaded Hardman to start production, and they gained their first joint commission for windows at Ushaw in November 1845. All the nineteenth-century stained glass in St Augustine's was executed by John Hardman & Co.

By Pugin's last illness all the tracery stained glass was in place, but in the church only the east window, the two south windows in the lady chapel, and the south west window were completed with stained glass lights, the remainder being fitted with plain quarries.[71] The balance of the stained glass lights was added later, the west window being the last to be completed in 1875. The later glass designs show a natural predilection for Benedictine saints. All windows in the

A Flint Seaside Church

church have equilateral arches, and use simple bar tracery, employing combinations of trefoil headed lancets, trefoils, quatrefoils, daggers and diamonds, similar to windows he installed at St Mary's, Brewood (1843) and St Peter's, Marlow (1845–48).

Plan

The plan is unusual for its apparent symmetry, both nave and chancel comprising two bays, the marginally shorter bays of the chancel resulting in the transept being slightly east of centre, in line with the tower. The south aisle and chapel are not substantially narrower than the nave and chancel. One-aisled churches are said to be a Kentish tradition, although only one in four of the remaining pre-fifteenth century north-east Kent churches has one side aisle. Pugin himself designed two other single-aisled churches at this period – St Peter's, Marlow and St Osmund's, Salisbury (1847–49). Both east and west elevations are in a straight line with separate gables to nave and aisle, a feature of many Kentish churches with equal length side-chapels and chancels, and one frequently employed by Pugin. The constrictions of the site, together with the importance Pugin placed on the sanctuary, resulted in the comparatively short nave. The southern transept contains the Pugin chantry, with the south porch nestled against its west wall.

The present north porch initially gave access directly to the nave, but was moved northwards when the west cloister was built. The original placing of the porch can be seen from the garth – unfortunately, the wall of the church was not made good with matching flint.

Dimensions

The nave is 8.6 metres long and 5.5 metres wide internally. The chancel is 8.5 metres long and 5.5 metres wide. The south aisle and lady chapel are the same length as the nave and chancel, the width being 4 metres. The transept measures 7 metres west to east. Pugin liked to work to a ratio of 3:2 for the length to width of nave, and this is fairly close to that proportion. The internal height of the nave is 9.7 metres, rather higher than would be given by Pugin's preferred height to width of nave ratio of 4:3. The internal height of the chancel is 9.9 metres, the south aisle 9.1 metres and the lady chapel 9.4 metres. Externally the nave is 13.1 metres high, the chancel 13.6 metres, the south aisle 11.8 metres, and the Pugin chantry 13.4 metres.

The Tower

The tower was to have been one stage taller, and topped by a spire, to form a landmark for passing vessels, in much the same way as the steeple at Birchington and the former spires at Reculver. Pugin appeared to have had difficulties deciding how the tower should be finished. One drawing, dated 1848, (in the library of

St Augustine's Church

6. PLAN OF ST AUGUSTINE'S, RAMSGATE, *based on a survey by W.F.J.Nicholson, Assoc. M Inst. C.E. (1941).*

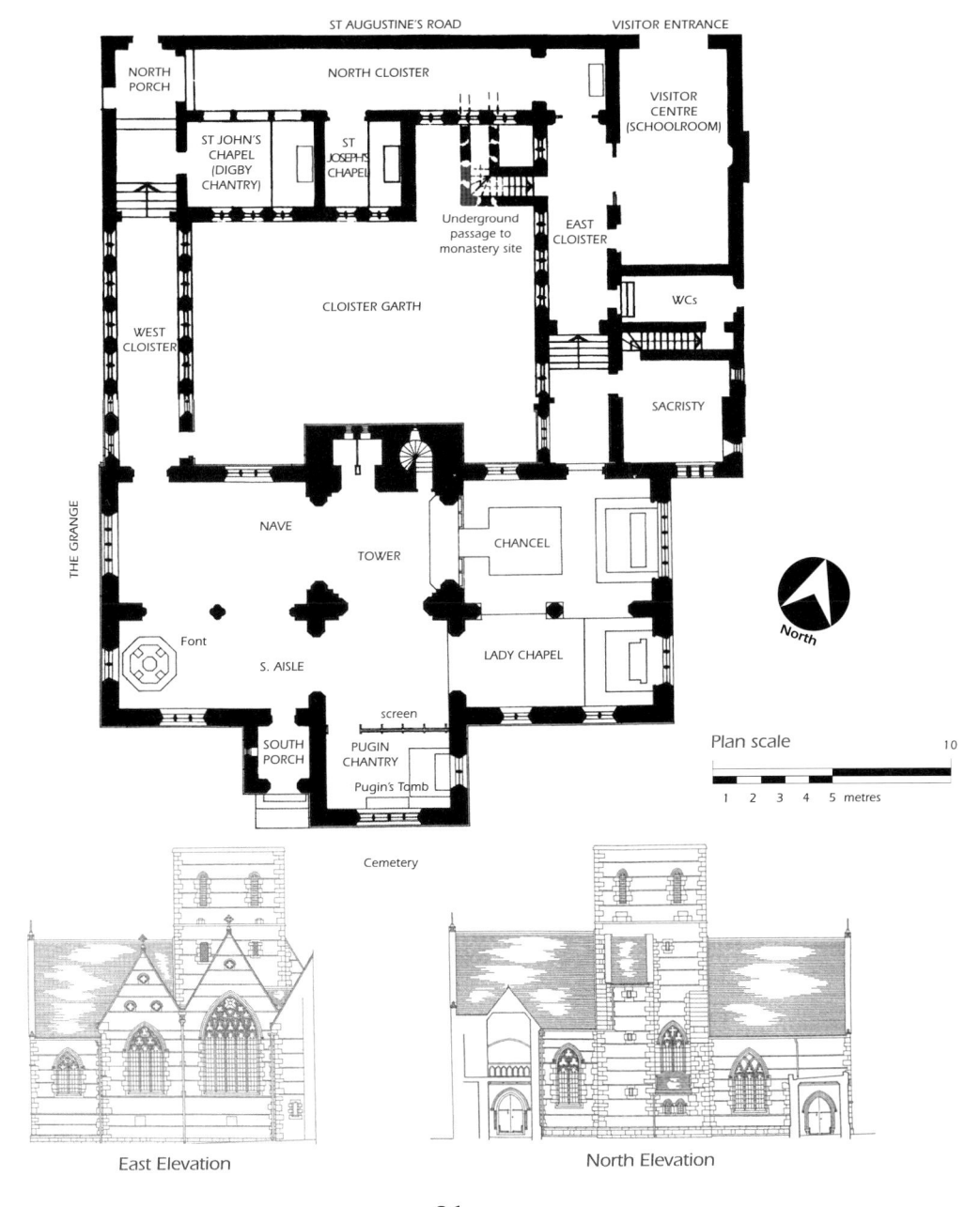

East Elevation

North Elevation

A Flint Seaside Church

the Royal Institute of British Architects) shows a broach spire, and Eastlake[72] contended that the spire was to be slate finished. The 1848 pen and ink perspective shows a two-light window on each face of the tower, but this design was dropped in favour of two plain single windows. In November 1850 there was a tremendous gale and Pugin obviously felt that the tower was in danger. To help reinforce the scaffolding, he sent for the crew of the *Caroline* who demanded immediate payment, £6 10s in all.[73]

Unfortunately, especially from an aesthetic point of view, the spire was not built at the time of Pugin's death, the tower merely boasting a lofty wooden crow's nest, visible to seamen from some distance. Although his sons Edward and Peter Paul extended the complex elsewhere, the tower and spire were never completed, which would have disappointed Pugin who advocated spires and denigrated flat towers, which he considered more suitable for defensive and domestic property.

7. St Augustine's Church, before 1860, viewed from the north

Schoolroom – now Visitor Centre

This was the first building on the site and was used as a temporary chapel until the main church was built, when it reverted to use as a schoolroom. It subsequently became part of the monastic community of the first monks, and was then fitted out as a sacristy in 1933 for Abbot Egan's Jubilee. The five-light north window, designed by Pugin and dating from 1846, depicts the Annunciation of Our Blessed Lady. Whilst the lower lights are of plain glass with a simple coloured border, the upper sections contain rich blues and yellows. The centre light depicts a vase (similar in style to some Pugin designed for the church and shown again in the Lady Chapel altar) containing white lilies, symbolic of the purity of the Virgin.

St Augustine's Church

East Cloister

The east cloister and associated buildings were the first to be completed. Now used as exhibition space, the cloister provides access to the schoolroom, the sacristy, chancel and an underground passage to the monastery site across the road. Above the junction of east and north cloisters rises the 18 metre high bell turret, with its lead-covered, timber-framed, pyramidal roof.

The style of the two-light stained glass windows in this cloister has been repeated in the newer additions. The yellow silver stain patterned quarries with coloured borders and central roundels may have been inspired by the thirteenth-century windows at St Mary, Chartham. Some of the designs, containing Kentish flowers, can be compared to those in *Floriated Ornament*. The stone tracery is almost identical to that Pugin designed for the school at Brewood (1843). There are two larger three-light windows in the southern end of the cloister. The cloister windows all date from 1846.[74] At the lower end of the cloister is a cupboard attributed to Edward Pugin.

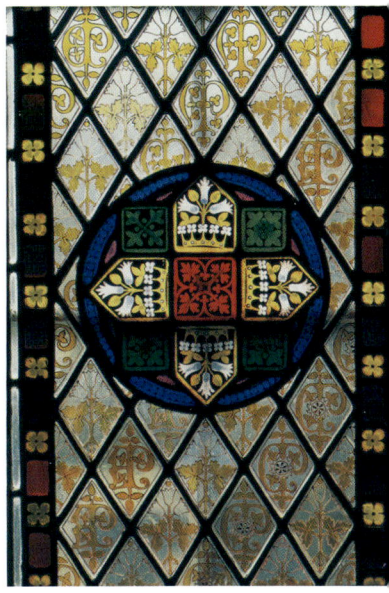

8. East cloister window, 1846, designed by Pugin

Sacristy

Beyond the gates across the east cloister, this wood-panelled room, originally intended as a small treasury, is heavily defended: the windows barred, and the splendid wooden door iron-plated on the inside. There is a magnificent Pugin-designed press, with sliding 'trays' for vestments, the doors faced with medieval linen-fold panels. The rectangular three-light south window dates from 1849.

Through the door into the sacristy, an opening to the left leads up to a set of steps arranged irregularly to give a medieval feel, to the Upper Sacristy, passing on the way two tiny windows possibly donated by Henri Gérente (1814–49), a stained glass artist from Paris. The glass is reputedly from the Sainte Chapelle, Paris, where Gérente, who once visited The Grange, did most of the glass restoration. The wooden vestment cupboard is attributed to Augustus Pugin. Passing through the organ loft, one turns right into a long room above the east cloister. This room has undergone a number of changes of use: it languished as a storage area, before being reordered as the Abbot's private chapel after World War II, a purpose which it held until the practice of private Masses was replaced with the option of concelebration. It has now reverted to a Library, as originally designed, and Study Room. The windows contain grisaille glass and exquisite sixteenth-century medallions of Flemish or German origin, which were obtained in 1847.

A Flint Seaside Church

9. Detail of sacristy window, 1846, designed by Pugin

North Cloister

The main entrance into the church is at the north-west corner of the cloister, next to St Edward's, originally the priest's house but now restored and converted to holiday accommodation by the Landmark Trust. A statue of St Augustine, flanked by the Benedictine motto 'Pax' and the arms of the Archbishopric of Canterbury, and carved in 1871 by R.L.Boulton of Cheltenham, guards the entrance. Pugin's hugely solid oak door includes a small wicket gate; in 1898, Paul Waterhouse noted that the entrance to the church was less than five feet high. Powell wrote that when people complained about the low lintels in the cloisters and church, Pugin replied 'The Faithful ought not to mind bending their heads when they enter a church; sightseers and heretics must take their chance'.[75]

At Pugin's death the roadside wall was built to a height of 76cm, the floor was laid, and the most easterly window facing the garth was installed (1846). The cloister, finally completed in 1860, was funded mainly by Kenelm Digby. Recent research attributes the design of this cloister to Edward Pugin.[76] The Stations of the Cross erected in March 1859 were replaced in 1893, although the original crosses can still be seen above the present painted terracotta Stations, which were created by the De Beule brothers of Ghent, in the style of their work in Flanders. They were re-painted in 1959 with a childlike brilliance. Brass plaques which cover the wall beneath the Stations commemorate deceased monks of the monastery. The monumental brass in the floor is dedicated to Father Wilfrid Alcock, the first Benedictine monk to arrive in Ramsgate, who was created an Abbot in 1872, and died in New Zealand in August 1882. Although this brass is not the work of Pugin, he did design at least 160 brasses which were made by Hardman's from 1841, and he was no doubt inspired by the wonderful early brasses which abound in the Kentish churches he visited. On the wall between the two chapels is a wooden

St Augustine's Church

panel commemorating the canonisation in 1935 of Sir Thomas More (1478–1535) and John Fisher (1469–1535), Bishop of Rochester.

Altar of the Sacred Heart
An altar of the Sacred Heart was erected in 1873, to be replaced by the present Peter Paul Pugin design sculpted by Boulton in the early 1880s at a cost of £400. Highly ornate and crocketted, it is a far cry from the simple Gothic style beloved by Pugin. The altar commemorates Father Alcock and was consecrated by the Rt Rev Dom Edmund Luck, one of the sons of Alfred Luck. The reredos depicts the Redeemer displaying his Sacred Heart to the faithful, with scenes from the life of St Margaret Mary Alacoque (1647–90) and St Gertrude the Great (c1256–1302) bearing a crozier, both prominent saints of the Sacred Heart devotion.

The encaustic floor tiles before the altar contain two decorated squares flanking a third square which depicts the Agnus Dei and an unusual design of dice representing the dice the centurions threw for Jesus' robe. The edging tiles depict the story (which recurs frequently throughout the church) of the raven carrying away the poisoned bread which was offered to St Benedict.

St Joseph's Chapel
In 1893 the Dowager Viscountess Southwell financed this chapel, probably designed by Peter Paul Pugin, to celebrate the coming of age of her son, Arthur. Well connected in Catholic circles, the dowager's brother was Francis Mostyn, who was created Vicar-Apostolic of Wales in 1895 and later Archbishop of Cardiff. The stained glass depicts Our Lady of Lourdes, St Joseph, St Theresa of Avila (1515–82) and St Michael. The altar, containing the relics of St Fortunatus and St Candida, is reputed to be by the De Beule brothers and shows the flight into Egypt; the reredos above depicts the death of St Joseph. A statuette of the seventh-century St Winifred of Wales stands in the chapel. The flooring is of plain red and white marble tiles, and the blue and gold gate is similar to that in the Digby Chantry, both gates echoing the lady chapel gates in the main church.

St John the Evangelist Chapel, or the Digby Chantry
This elaborate chapel, in the corner of the west and north cloisters, costing £2,500, was financed by Kenelm Digby, author of the celebrated *Broad Stone of Honour*, and designed by Edward Pugin.[77] Above the entrance is carved the Digby crest containing the unusual emblem of an ostrich holding a horseshoe, with the motto *Deo non fortuna* (By God, not chance). Digby, a fellow Roman Catholic convert, and friend of Pugin, rented No 2 Royal Crescent in Ramsgate from 1851–56. (Shrewsbury was recommended by Pugin to take No 1 when visiting Ramsgate.) The leaf-form gates are medieval in spirit, separating people from, yet allowing them close proximity to, the objects of veneration.

A Flint Seaside Church

Powell designed all the stained glass. The east window depicts the Last Judgement, the central light showing Christ seated within a circular rainbow (symbolising God's Covenant with Man). On the altar below, consecrated by Bishop Grant on St Benedict's Day, 1859, is a relic of the boy martyr St Benignus transferred here from the catacombs of St Priscilla in 1859, together with relics of St Florentina (d c636) and St Arista.

The other windows depict the name saints of the Digby family: the Virgin Mary, the martyred boy King St Kenelm (d821), St Jane of Valois (1461–1504), St Marcella of Rome (325–410), St John the Evangelist, and Thomas the Apostle. Dom Bede Millard OSB noted Powell's close observation of nature in the varying size of lily leaves on the stem held by St Kenelm. The names of those buried in the Chantry are inscribed on tablets between the windows – Digby's children, John Gerald (1847–56) and Thomas (1835–56); his wife Jane Mary (d1860) and his mother-in-law Marcella Dillon (d1860). Kenelm Digby himself was buried at St Mary's, Kensal Green.

In 1884 Bishop Coffin named Our Lady of Sorrows as the secondary patron of the church, in honour of the pietà in this chapel. This was recorded in the inscription on the former high altar.

West Cloister

This cloister, now also attributed to Edward Pugin, and built in 1859, has a flat roof of which Pugin would have totally disapproved. Just before the entrance to the church is a fine brass, dated 1864, dedicated to the Rev Alfred Luck OSB who requested to be buried at the entrance to the church so that all who entered might think of him and pray for him. Luck gave regular donations to the church, including the building of the entire west cloister. A widower, he lived in The Grange, when the family moved to Birmingham following Pugin's death, and later built St Gregory's (now demolished) in the Monastery grounds. Luck became a Benedictine monk and was ordained priest at Subiaco in February 1861; his sons, John Edmund (d1896) and Francis Augustine (d1899), joined the monastery, the former becoming the first Bishop of Auckland, New Zealand; and a daughter, Mary, became a Benedictine nun. Beyond the delightful cloister windows a door gives access to the garth.

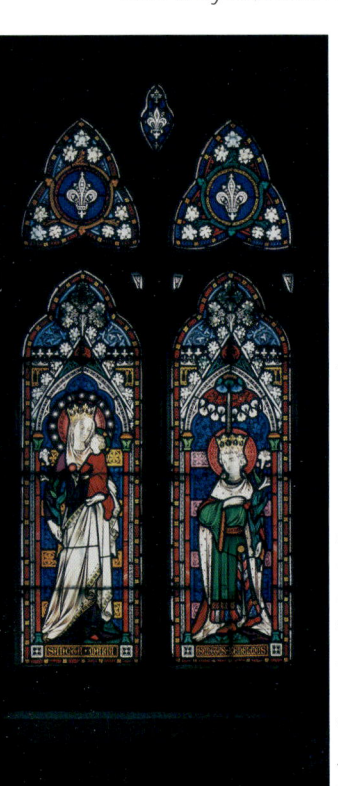

10. Window in Digby Chantry, designed by John Hardman Powell, showing the Virgin Mary and King St Kenelm

St Augustine's Church

The Garth

This quadrangle is asymmetrical and has a distinctly medieval aura to it, with the juxtaposition of various roofs, buttresses and uneven disposition of windows. The fanciful gargoyles, though not all to Pugin's design, are reminiscent of the imaginative creations to be found at St Martin's, Herne, where the huge-eared creatures, lions' heads and woodwose (a man of the woods) were probably the inspiration for similar carvings at St Augustine's.

Huddled against the north wall of the chancel are old crosses, one of which, dedicated to Captain Isan Thomaso and two fellow seamen, Noel Thomaso and Jean Marie Phillippe, bears a bas-relief of a boat. Sadly the elements have taken their toll and the design can no longer be deciphered, but Pugin's sketch survives in a private collection. The men were drowned when their ship foundered during a heavy gale on 21 October 1846 and Pugin had their bodies carried to St Augustine's for burial, the first to be conducted in Thanet according to Catholic ritual, since the sixteenth century.

A lean-to roof in the north east corner of the garth covers the steps down to a passage which leads from the east cloister, under the road, to the Abbey. This was constructed in 1863, originally ending at the Sacred Heart altar, but lengthened to its present position in 1875. It not only protected the monks in days of anti-Catholic feeling, but also supported their monastic rule of enclosure.

Nave

Pugin was usually vehement in his support of a south porch as the main entrance to a church. Perhaps he felt that the passage to the east of the church, giving access to the churchyard and thence to the south porch, was too slight, and therefore placed the main entrance to the north, opening directly into the nave. The label stops above the doorway represent St Benedict and his sister St Scholastica. The carvings throughout the church are a delight, mainly depicting saints, although there are some knots of foliage, and, protecting the tower crossing, lion heads reminiscent of those at St Martin's, Herne.

The two-bay nave is elongated by the transept crossing. The pillars forming the tower support are huge in dimension and asymmetrical. The single pillar in the nave, and that in the chancel are both quatrefoil in plan, a simple design motif which Pugin frequently employed. There is a pleasing dissimilarity in the sec-

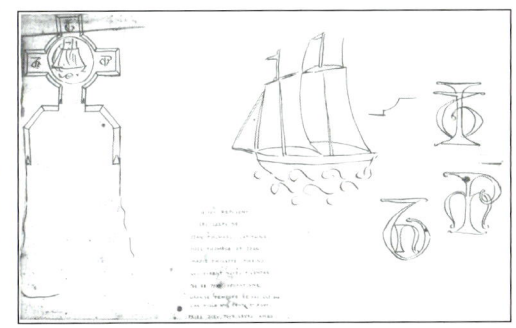

11. Pugin's sketch for Isan Thomaso's tombstone, 1846

A Flint Seaside Church

tions of the columns, some rounded, others severely angled, as there is also in the form of mouldings, a definite medieval trait. Twelve consecration crosses are carved at various intervals round the walls. It was originally intended to panel the nave ceiling, but the scissor-beam oak roof structure remains as it was at the time of Pugin's death, and accords with many of the local thirteenth and fourteenth-century Kentish churches. The floor is of black and red tiles. Near the entrance is one of the original wooden poor boxes made by Hardman.

The tracery stained glass of the four-light west window dates from 1849, whilst the lower lights were installed in 1875 at a cost of £88 10s 2d. The clarity and brightness of colour in the older glass is shown to advantage against the Powell lights,

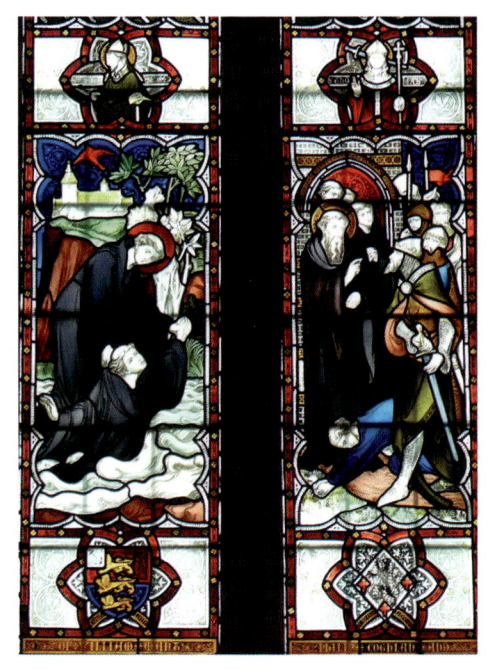

12. The west window, showing two episodes from the life of St Benedict (detail)

which depict the following scenes from the life of St Benedict: the saint plunging into a thicket of thorns to overcome a temptation of the flesh; a raven with bread in its beak; the saint talking to St Scholastica during a miraculous rain storm; dying before the altar; in the company of his young disciple St Maurus; St Maurus saving the child Placid from drowning; St Benedict talking to King Totila; and seeing the soul of St Germanus, Bishop of Capua (d c545) carried to heaven by angels. The inscription reads "Pray for the good estate of William Mant Philip Coghlan and Mary Joseph, his wife". The family arms are shown in the lower lights, together with those of St Benedict and the Cassinese Benedictine Congregation of the Primitive Observance.

Above the window are small quatrefoil glazed openings used to ventilate the church, and remarked upon by *The Builder* in 1852. Similar ventilators can be seen on the south wall of the chantry and the east wall of the lady chapel, and illustrate Pugin's practical approach. Practicality is again in evidence in the small sloping grooves in each window sill ending in a drainage hole intended to carry away condensation. The wall below the west window is panelled with wood to a height of about two metres. The modern stone statue of St Anthony of Padua (1195–1231) and the Holy Child was carved by Philip Lindsey Clark. The tracery stained

St Augustine's Church

13. St Augustine's looking towards the chancel:
pen and watercolour by A.W.N.Pugin, c1850

A Flint Seaside Church

glass in the three-light window on the north wall of the nave was originally installed early in 1849, but replaced later in the year, and the middle trefoil probably dates from 1868. The lights commemorate the death of Matilda Mary Coghlan in 1867. Three Benedictine abbesses are depicted – St Gertrude the Great, St Mechtilde of Magdeburg (c1210–c1280) carrying her book of visions and St Mildred (d c700) with her fawn. Legend tells that the king granted St Mildred the lands enclosed by the tracks of a fawn for Minster Abbey, of which her mother Domneva was consecrated first abbess in 669. The saints' habits are created from a wonderful dark purple glass silhouetted against a rich ruby red – a stunning and most unusual effect. The statue before the transept is of St Benedict, again accompanied by a raven.

Pugin's practical turn of mind and attention to detail is shown in the instructions he gave Crace for a chair for the confessional. 'It should be ... plain but of this form ... a good width and length on the elbows as the priest has to rest his head on his arm ... it should be covered with strong leather'.[78] The single-light confessional windows, diapered and with small floriated roundels, cost £8 for the pair, and date from 1849. Pugin was obviously delighted with these windows, commenting to Hardman that 'the glass used in the quarries has the silvery look ... be sure you make all leafwork of geometrical windows of this glass it is quite lovely'.[79] Above the confessional, in the transept, is a two-light window which was probably installed in 1849 and depicts St Catherine of Alexandria and St Margaret of Antioch. There are also two statues in this area, one of St Joseph above the confessional, and another of St Augustine holding a model of the church surmounted with tabernacle work, designed by Pugin.

A change in colour of ashlar indicates where a Caen stone pulpit once stood, donated by a Miss Burchall in 1869. In 1877 a visitor noted that the priest left the nave through the confessional, from which a small spiral staircase led to the pulpit, the entrance covered with a scarlet hanging. To judge from the remaining front panel of the pulpit (showing the Sermon on the Mount), now in the Cartoon Room at The Grange, the pulpit must have been rather out of scale with the rest of the church.

Pugin was a tireless advocate for the re-introduction of rood screens, arguing that:

14. Watercolour by Pugin of the confessionals under construction, c1849

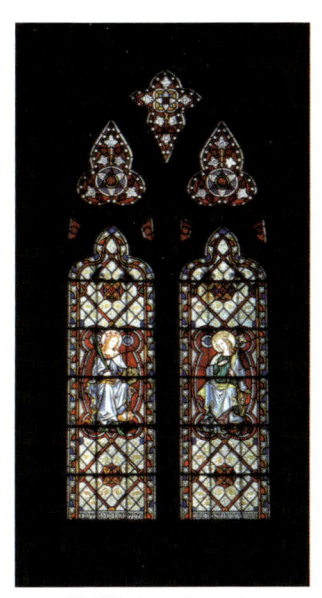

St Augustine's Church

the place where this most holy sacrifice is to be offered up, should be set apart and railed off from less ordered parts of the church, and we find this to have been the case in all ages, in all styles, and in all countries professing the catholic faith down to a comparatively very recent period.[80]

The five-bay fifteenth-century style oak rood screen with ornately cusped ogee arches and carved crockets, made by Myers, was moved to the lady chapel after a re-organisation of the church in 1970. In 2016 the screen was returned to its original position with the rood fixed above it.[81]

There is much speculation concerning the crucifix. Pugin's pen and watercolour drawing of the interior of the church looking towards the chancel shows a trefoil-ended crucifix with attendant figures of Our Lady and St John, whereas the present one has fleur-de-lys finials. The cross is thought to be fourteenth-century with a fifteenth-century figure of Christ, and could conceivably have been brought to England from the Netherlands by Pugin in the *Caroline*.

15. Window above the confessional, designed by Pugin, showing St Catherine of Alexandria and St Margaret of Antioch

Chancel

A step leads into the two-bay chancel where the ceiling is panelled and decorated with gilded bosses. The floor is laid with Minton encaustic patterned tiles, with plain black and red tiles in the choir. The choir stalls have been returned to their original positions. A further step raises the sanctuary, where the altar, although separated from the congregation by the rood screen, was designed to be the focal point of the church and its services. The altar, as existing in 1884, was composed of four grey marble shafts with ornamented capitals supporting a solid Caen stone mensa upon which were engraved the following words:

> Deo in hon. S. Augustinu Ep. et SS. VII. dolor. B.M.V. hanc aram atq. Eccles. dicavit Robertus Ep. Southwarcen. XVII. Cal. Aug. MDCCCLXXXIV solemniis cum. indulg. plen. in posterum Dom. I. post Cal. Aug. recolend.[82]

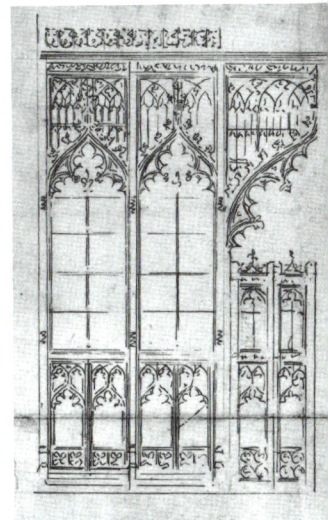

16. Pugin's design for the rood screen at St Augustine's, c1850

A Flint Seaside Church

17. The choir and rood screen seen from the east

Despite its artistic importance, this altar was destroyed during the 1970 re-ordering, but a new altar has been created based on that design. It incorporates the relic of St Augustine, together with those of St Gregory the Great and St Laurence of Canterbury. Old photographs show upon the altar the 4.9 metre towering stone tabernacle and throne, which were originally made for the Great Exhibition in 1851. Opinions vary as to whether the tabernacle was ever meant for St Augustine's, and it certainly detracted from the east window.[83] It was removed as part of the re-ordering and is now to be found in the Harvard Chapel in the Anglican Southwark Cathedral. A smaller tabernacle has now been installed.

The two-light window on the north wall, dating from 1850, was presented by John Knill (1824–98), a relation of the third Mrs Pugin. He became a Catholic in 1844 and, together with his wife Elizabeth, is buried in the churchyard. The window depicts St John of Beverley (d721) and St Elizabeth of Hungary (1207–31). John Newman suggests that the precedent for the magnificent five-light east window was the west window at St Nicholas-at-Wade.[84] Pugin used similar elongated, pointed trefoils in the tracery of the east window, St Mary's Cathedral, Newcastle-upon-Tyne (c1844) and in the west window of St Osmund's, Salisbury (1847). The window measures 6 x 3.6 metres, the tracery stained glass dating from 1848, and the lights 1849. The theme is that of the *Te Deum* with Christ in Glory in the centre surrounded by angels with scrolls bearing verses from the *Te Deum*, and the Lamb of God above. The four Evangelists are represented at the base of the window, and the whole is cleverly linked by a grape vine which weaves its way round the figures.

Below the stone arcading of the organ chamber a large door gives access into the east cloister. The original organ, a two-manual instrument, was

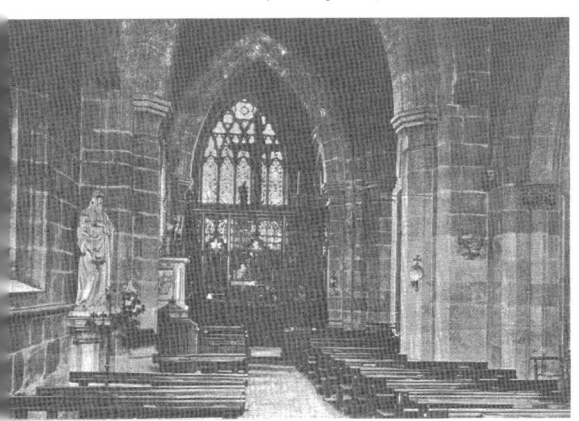

18. View looking towards the chancel, showing the carved stone pulpit of 1869

St Augustine's Church

purchased by Pugin in 1847, and placed in the gallery where the organ pipes are now situated. An entry in the account book for 6 August reads 'Carriage organ and organ £113 8s 1d'.[85] In 1948 a former theatre organ was purchased and, together with its three-manual console was placed behind the lady chapel altar, with the pipes in the organ loft. F. H. Browne & Sons rebuilt the organ in 1982 to provide thirty-five speaking stops together with manual and pedal couplers. The stops and soundboard on the great manual were taken from the original Pugin organ and remain to this day. In 2016 the organ was restored by Henry Willis & Sons. A new console was built and located in the west of the lady chapel.

Lady Chapel

Separated from the chancel by parclose screens, the lady chapel has a wood-panelled ceiling and floor laid with Minton encaustic tiles, the sanctuary area marked by blue, yellow and white fleur-de-lys. Contributors to the Pugin Memorial of 1860 commissioned the gold and blue gated screen, featuring fleur-de-lys and naturalistic lilies. Designed by Powell, its flowing, sinuous line is characteristic of his drawing style, but as translated into wrought iron looks almost Art Nouveau. It gained a prize at the 1862 International Exhibition, and is so well constructed and balanced that it opens noiselessly.

    The beautifully carved stone altar, which has now been moved back to its original position, depicts the Annunciation, Nativity and Epiphany, and was made by Myers to Pugin's design in thanksgiving for the recovery of his daughter, Anne, is backed by wrought iron riddels topped by candlesticks, of the same pattern as the gates. Above the altar is a three-light window. Appreciating that Pugin was unhappy with the tracery stained glass installed in 1848, Hardman introduced new lights and tracery in 1853 at a cost of £45. The present lights, designed by Powell and fitted in 1861 at a cost of £60, were a gift from the Pugin Memorial Committee. The window, in which blues predominate, depicts Our Lady crushing the head of a serpent, surrounded by the figures of St Agnes (d c350) holding a Lamb, St Catherine of Alexandria with a wheel, St Anne, Eve, St Jane of Valois, and St Margaret of Antioch overcoming a dragon, and so incorporates the names of all Pugin's female relations. The lower part of the window shows Christ and the Burning Bush, and Powell followed Pugin's example by linking the pictorial elements with a spreading foliage of lilies.

    The south windows were designed by Pugin, the tracery glass being executed in 1848 and the lights 1851. The windows were exhibited in the Mediæval Court at the 1851 Great Exhibition, where the rich blue glass was much admired, and were donated to the church by Hardman. Simple two-light windows, the first depicts scenes from the life of Our Lady, including the Annunciation, the Visitation, the Birth of Christ, and the Adoration of the Magi. The second window shows the Presentation in the Temple, the Flight into Egypt, the Dormition of Mary, and her

A Flint Seaside Church

Coronation in Heaven. One image is especially significant: the pillar with the broken statue represents the idols of Egypt bowing down as the Holy Family pass by, a reference to arcane medieval texts with which, in the 1840s, few would have been conversant.

A stone carving by Myers of the Virgin and Child, with metal crowns, placed on the wall between the lady chapel and Pugin chantry, is a copy of one made for St David's at Pantasaph which was exhibited at the 1851 Great Exhibition. Fleur-de-lys tiles have been placed beneath the statue. The silver lamp, hanging to the left of these figures, in the form of a fourteenth-century 'church ship', is a copy of the original, which was unfortunately stolen.

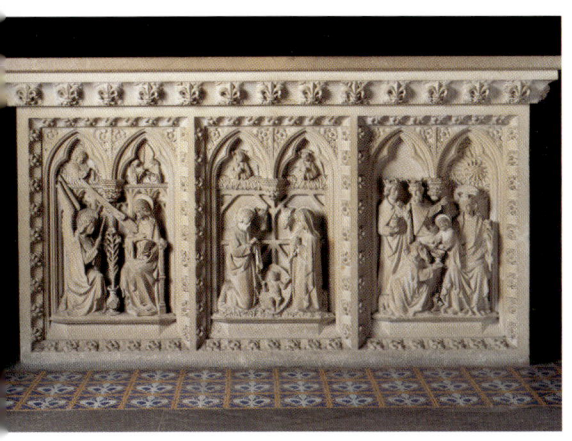

19. Carved stone altar in the lady chapel, designed by Pugin

20. Virgin and Child, designed by Pugin and sculpted by George Myers (detail)

- 34 -

St Augustine's Church

21. The Pugin chantry: 'If there is a crown for honesty and a crown for ardour, if there are wreaths for truth, honesty, simplicity and toil, we can bring them and lay them on his tomb.'
(Paul Waterhouse, *Architectural Review*, Vol 3, 1897)

A Flint Seaside Church

Pugin Chantry or the Chapel of St Laurence and St Stephen

One enters the chantry through a five-bay, Perpendicular style, carved oak parclose screen, which lacks the delicacy and lightness of the rood screen. The tomb of Augustus Welby Pugin lies beneath the south window. According to Powell, Pugin delighted in the tombs and monuments of great men in the public squares in Italy; and there are many fine examples of tombs and mausolea in the Kentish churches with which he was familiar, particularly St Nicholas, Ash. Pugin also boasted to Bloxam in 1840 that he made the 'first recumbent ecclesiastical effigy',[86] presumably since the Reformation. Pugin's effigy shows a man 5ft 5in tall, dressed in a simple medieval garment, and with his feet resting on two martlets. Straight hair frames the clean-shaven face with high forehead and rounded, rather sensual lips, but the keen grey eyes everyone remarked upon have lost their restless and penetrating gaze. Paul Waterhouse noted the 'rather stumpy hands, with short, nimble fingers'.[87] The slab under the effigy is marked as if intended for inscription and below this, Pugin's family as weepers are carved in niches. On the wall behind the effigy are alabaster slabs, decorated with entwined roses and martlets, and with a plain central roundel. The base of the tomb is completed with specially produced Minton tiles bearing the legend: PRAY FOR THE SOUL OF AUGUSTUS WELBY PUGIN THE FOUNDER OF THIS CHURCH. The tomb, made by Myers in 1852–3, is one of Edward Pugin's first independent designs.[88]

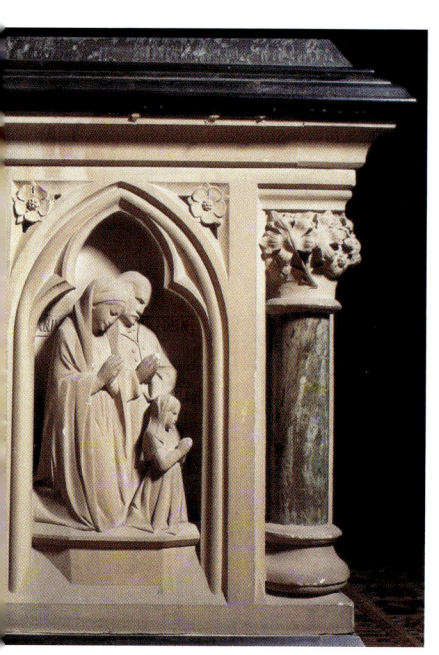

22. Detail from Pugin's tomb: his daughter Anne, her husband John Hardman Powell, and their daughter Mildred

Twelve members of the Pugin family are buried in the vault below the Chantry, the details of ten of them being displayed in the family tree (see page 53). Two children of his daughter Agnes are also buried here, commemorated by brasses to the left of the altar, namely Augustus Lewis Edward John who died aged 6 months on 30 August 1869, and was buried by Dom C Sanders OSB on 1 September; and Augusta Annette Emma who died aged 4 months on 17 August 1872, and was buried by John Edmund Luck OSB on 21 August 1872. The vault also holds the remains of Edmund (Dom Benignus Mary) Sullivan OSB who died on 30 October 1865 and was buried in November of that year by his brother Dom Adalbert Sullivan OSB. The last burial was that of Cuthbert Pugin in 1928. The vault was opened on 29 October 1992, as a result of concern about cracks which had

St Augustine's Church

23. Tiles from the Pugin Chantry

24. Tiles also from the Pugin Chantry, showing the family crest – the martlet – and the monogram 'AWP'

A Flint Seaside Church

appeared in the alabaster slabs behind Pugin's effigy. The vault, measuring 4.6 metres north-south, and 4.3 metres east-west has a brick arch ceiling reaching a height of 1.9 metres. The coffins, each consisting of three chests, the inner and outer ones being composed of wood and the middle one of lead, were placed on and below a stone shelf. Dom Bede noted that most of the coffins were trapezoid with gabled lids, many of the fittings (by Hardman) were gold plated, and the handles locked at a 45 degree angle ensuring that the bearers' knuckles would not be crushed. Gilded and enamelled floriated crosses decorate the length of Pugin's and Jane's coffins.[89]

The four-light south window above Pugin's tomb has tracery stained glass dating from 1849, the large quatrefoil depicting St Louis. The lights, commissioned by J.Lambert at a cost of £100, were not added until 1861. Dedicated to the life of St Augustine, they portray: St Gregory the Great meeting Anglo-Saxon slaves; dispatching St Augustine to England; St Augustine landing in Thanet; preaching to King St Ethelbert of Kent (560–616); processing with his monks to Canterbury; saying Mass at St Martin's, Canterbury; baptising King St Ethelbert; and laying the foundation stone for St Augustine's Abbey, Canterbury. The lower part of the window shows Pugin himself, dressed as a Benedictine oblate, together with his three wives. The scene showing St Gregory and St Augustine uses streaky glass to represent marble, apparently the first time the technique had been used since the Middle Ages.[90]

The gilded and painted Caen stone altar originally stood in Pugin's private chapel at The Grange, but was moved here in the 1930s. Pugin's predilection for carving the front of altars is unusual, since medieval ones tended to be plain stone.

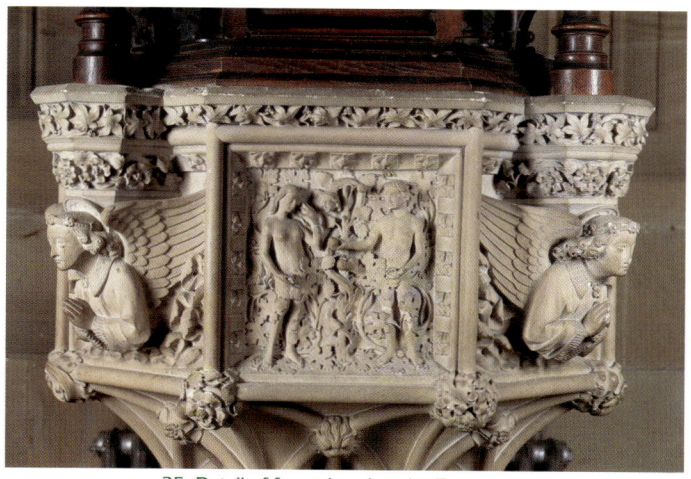

25. Detail of font, showing the Temptation

St Augustine's Church

A piscina is placed in the wall to the south. Sir John Sutton Bt, a friend of Pugin and fellow convert, donated the painting, which is thought to be by August Martin (1837-1901), a German Gothic Revival artist. Although in the style of fifteenth-century Flemish works, it is contemporary with the date of the church.[91] The central panel shows Our Lady of Pity with the dead body of Christ, in the company of St John and St Mary Magdalene. The left hand panel shows St Augustine, whilst the right panel shows St Michael weighing a Christian against three demons and a castle, in much the same way that, in Contrasts Pugin depicted a Gothic cathedral balanced against classical buildings, the latter being found wanting.

The two-light east window, executed in 1849, depicts the patron saints of the chapel, St Laurence of Rome (d258) and St Stephen the Protomartyr (d c35). The Minton encaustic tiling shows Pugin's monogram and the martlet, with a border of intertwined martlets and foliage; the style makes an attribution to Edward Pugin most likely. The chantry is wood panelled to dado level. The wrought iron votive candlestick was made by Hardman and exhibited at the 1851 Great Exhibition. John Tallis considered that it was intended for the lady chapel, and was fulsome in his praise, describing it as 'a most elaborate piece of iron-work, worthy of the ancient smiths ... striking proof that our operations, when under proper directions, are quite capable of representing the most beautiful works of medieval skill'.[92]

South Aisle

Although the tracery glass in the three-light window near the font dates from 1849, the lights were not added until 1861. The window depicts Benedictine Saints: Bede of Jarrow (673–735), the author of *A History of the English Church and People* (731); St Wilfrid (633–709), Archbishop of York; and St Cuthbert (d687), one of Bede's scholars and later Abbot of Wearmouth and Jarrow. Commissioned by Luck, at a cost of £35, it commemorates the first three Benedictines to work in Kent since the Reformation, Father Bede Whiteside, Father Wilfrid Alcock, and Father Cuthbert Downey (Pro-Vicar of Bengal 1875–78, died 1895).

26. Engraving of font from the 1851 Great Exhibition Catalogue

A Flint Seaside Church

The two-light west window of the baptistry has tracery glass dating from 1849 and lights made in 1851. This exquisite, delicately coloured, window shows King Ethelbert, who was converted by Augustine, and his wife Queen St Bertha (d612), under canopied tabernacle work. In an article on the 1851 Great Exhibition, it was rightly noted that:

> the richness of the two principal figures is well relieved by a white ground; and this style of glass, treated on the old principles, has all the advantages of producing a rich effect, without impeding the sufficiency of light from entering the edifice.[93]

The window was a gift from Pugin's friend, the painter J.R.Herbert RA, (1810–90) who, through Pugin's influence, converted to Catholicism in 1840. A rose window of four linked quatrefoils, dated 1849, is placed high in the west wall.

The spectacular font, probably inspired by the Seven Sacrament Font at Little Walsingham, Norfolk, was exhibited at the 1851 Great Exhibition where it was greatly admired by Queen Victoria and Prince Albert. The base and steps are carved from a single block of Caen stone and the octagonal bowl, a favoured thirteenth-century shape, is decorated with carvings representing the Temptation, St John Preaching in the Wilderness, the Baptism of Christ, and the Crucifixion, the panels divided by figures of angels which act as supports to the canopy. The Evangelists, St John the Baptist, St Peter, St Paul, and the Virgin Mary are sculpted on the pedestal. The practice of covering fonts to prevent holy water being stolen for witchcraft, developed into an art form, the late fourteenth-century carpenters producing immensely tall spires of carved and pierced oak tabernacle work. When the font is to be used the cover is lifted into the canopy by a counter-weight pulley system, forming a ceiling with the Holy Dove in the centre.

The painting over the south door, depicting Our Lady with the Holy Child, and the figures of St Augustine and St Thomas of Canterbury (1118–70), was commissioned from the German painter, Platner, by a novice of the Society of Jesus in 1857.[94] The panel was subsequently presented to the Diocese of Southwark with the request that it should be placed above an altar dedicated to St Augustine. Pugin's pen and watercolour interior perspective shows a niche in this position.

South Porch

The south porch of a Pugin church is usually a treat, and this lean-to porch is therefore rather a disappointment in its vernacular understatement. Equipped with a holy water-stoup on the east side, stone benches, and a flooring of incised tiles, it is redeemed by a lively carving on the west side of the portal of a woodwose, complete with bulging eyes, comparable with one at St Martin's, Herne. New gates now provide extra security.

St Augustine's Church

27. View of the church and The Grange in the late 1850s, engraved by O. Jewitt, from Benjamin Ferrey's *Recollections of A.N.Welby Pugin*, 1861

28. Similar view of the same site in 2016

A Flint Seaside Church

Churchyard

The best views of the church can be gained from the churchyard. The exterior is uncompromisingly plain, with little apparent roof or wall articulation. It can be seen from the gable ends, adorned with floriated crosses, that Pugin adhered to his own principles, in that the sides form an equilateral triangle – 'the most beautiful pitch'.[95] Access to the churchyard can also be gained from the road, to the east of the church. This narrow strip of land was purchased from Matthew Habershon, a 'repulsive humbug',[96] on 10 March 1850 for the extortionate sum of £283 10s 0d.

29. The Grange – 'convenient and solid' – drawn by Pugin, letter to Bloxam

The churchyard cross commemorates the Rev Thomas Costigan who baptised several of the Pugin children and celebrated mass in the church. Pugin probably found his height intimidating – 6ft 5in – and certainly found his unsophisticated manners irritating. In the south west corner of the churchyard can be found the graves of the Abbey monks. Three of Anne Hardman Powell's children are buried in grave 232 (on right side of path leading from south porch to sea – near church): James Kenelm Pugin Powell who died on 29 October 1924 and was buried by Dom Anselm Fox OSB (d 1928); Cecilia Powell who died 17 July 1925 and was buried on 23 July also by Dom Fox; and Dunstan John Powell who died 20 March 1932 and was buried on 23 March by Abbot Erkenwald Egan OSB (d1939).

THE GRANGE (1843–44) Restored by the Landmark Trust, 2006

Standing in the churchyard, one can see Habershon's flint faced row of houses to the east, beyond which is West Cliff Lodge (originally named Royal Villa) and the Royal Crescent. To the west is a buff coloured brick building with stone dressings, steeply sloping slate roofs, and a lookout tower, 3.7 metres square and 15 metres high. This is The Grange, Pugin's family home, built at a cost of £3,500. Pugin argued that this amount was justified for work 'so completely finished and carried out',[97] probably referring to the wainscot in the dining room, the stone fireplaces in each room, the stained glass in upper sections of the windows, the wallpaper and the upholstery. One account from Crace, dated 1846, includes the following items:

St Augustine's Church

> To 6 chairs, the backs stuffed with best curled hair in fine canvas, with elastic spring stuffed seats covered in crimson Utrecht velvet trimmed with silk tufts and gymp and finished with gothic brass nails. Each £3 18s
> To a furniture for a French Bedstead of green striped Merino, bound with silk Parisian binding £4 18s 6d
> To two Curtains of rich marone and gold Tapestry, bound with gold color silk figured lace and finished at bottom with marone and gold trellio fringe £8 3s 6d[98]

Although it was regarded as something of a curiosity by holiday-makers, Pugin was obviously immensely proud of his house, assuring Griffiths that *'it is the only home in the Island fit to receive a Bishop'*.[97] The delightful quick sketch, sent to Bloxam, shows that, even at this early stage, Pugin knew exactly what he was going to build, even down to the arrangement of windows.

After the idiosyncrasies of his first house, St Marie's Grange, near Salisbury, this dwelling is eminently practical, designed to accommodate a large family and staff, as well as a study, and a chapel. The 1851 census notes that the household consisted of Pugin and his wife Jane, five children (Cuthbert was presumably at school, Anne was already married to J.H.Powell, and Peter Paul was born later that year), and four servants, of whom three came from Staffordshire, where Pugin had many commissions. The 1871 census records that Edward, Cuthbert, Peter Paul and Jane Pugin were living at The Grange served by a total of six servants. Father Jauch remarked on the:

> splendid windows, which admit abundance of light into the spacious rooms, but you will never perceive the slightest draught, however close to the windows or doors you may place yourself, and you will even find a clever contrivance by which the drops on the condensing panes are safely carried outside the building.[100]

The entrance to The Grange is from St Augustine's Road, past gateposts guarded by two huge stone lions, additions of Edward Pugin. To the right is the cartoon room, used for the preparation of stained glass designs, and filled with medieval artefacts intended to inspire the artists. The extravagant glazed corridor, which stretches across the paved courtyard was another of Edward Pugin's additions. The range of buildings to the left housed a larder, scullery, kitchen and store. Some extensions and enlargements by Edward Pugin were removed in the 2006 restoration. The interior is well laid out, with spacious rooms and a double-height entrance hall, with unusual banisters on the staircase and gallery, similar to Chinese lattice work, but probably based on timber designs Pugin discovered in Abbeville, France, and which he used to illustrate *Details of Ancient Timber Houses of the Fifteenth and Sixteenth Centuries* (1836). The hall gives access to the draw-

A Flint Seaside Church

ing room (7.3 x 4.3 metres), the library (8.5 x 4.6 metres) with bay window, and the large dining room (8.5 x 4.3 metres) which boasts a magnificent fireplace and inglenook under an oak beam. The stone-mullioned casement windows were fitted with quarried glass except on the south, where plate glass was used to take advantage of the views, but with stained glass above the transoms to provide colour and decoration. To the east are the sacristy and private chapel (5.1 x 2.7 metres) fitted out with Minton tiles and stained glass by Wailes.

On the first floor there are now four large bedrooms with fireplaces. Pugin allowed for one bathroom on this floor and another in the tower where there is a further bedroom, once occupied by J.H.Powell. The tower itself, with lead covered roof, and battlemented parapet, provided Pugin with a look-out. One can picture him on stormy days, standing there, dressed in sou'wester, his telescope trained on vessels approaching the harbour, 'watching each "come in" with intense interest how "they answered their helms", and the sails were managed, until the critical sweep of the tide was safely over'.[101]

In the hall of The Grange a door gives access to a tunnel which once terminated in a chamber in the cliff face. This was destroyed in a cliff fall in 1947. Whether Pugin inherited these passages or created new ones is unclear.

30. & 31. Details of the doorway to St Edward's, left hand side, and below, right hand side

ST EDWARD'S PRESBYTERY Restored by the Landmark Trust, 2015

Despite the '1849' carved on the right hand side of its entrance, Pugin did not begin work on St Edward's until 1850. The accounts detail the purchase of timber for what was then termed the verger's house. The monks lived here before the monastery was built. The dwelling, now providing holiday accommodation, had direct access into the west cloister, which used to be the private right of way for the Pugin family. The oriel window over St Augustine's Road, first indicated in Pugin's sketch to Hardman (p.46) was an addition by Edward Pugin, of 1863.

ST AUGUSTINE'S ABBEY A Benedictine monastery until 2011, now the Divine Retreat Centre of the Vincentian Fathers of Kerala, Marymatha Province, India.

St Benedict, the founder of the order, was born in Umbria in 480 AD and sent to Rome by his parents to complete his education. Leaving the city, he settled at Subiaco, in the mountains east of Rome. The monastic order which he founded

St Augustine's Church

there was based on a simple, ordered way of life, set out in his *Rule*. Each monastery was a religious family, providing for its own needs, supporting dependants, offering hospitality and spiritual succour, but essentially serving God without contact with the world.

In 1849 James Hayes Alcock, who was born in Lancashire in 1831, travelled to Genoa to join Abbot Peter Casaretto's house of the Cassinese Congregation of Benedictine monks and took the name of Father Wilfrid Alcock. Pressure from

32. St Augustine's Monastery in 1875, before it became an Abbey in 1896: sepia pen and ink drawing, probably by Cuthbert Welby Pugin

Thomas Grant (1816–70), first Bishop of Southwark, to establish a mission in southern England led Casaretto to send Alcock to Ramsgate in 1855 to report on the situation. According to Don Luigi Massa, a priest in London who acted as intermediary between Grant and Casaretto, Grant wanted:

> Benedictines at Ramsgate, if for no other reason, because Pugin had said before dying that this was his intention. If Pugin had lived a little longer and had had at his side a person interested in the Benedictines, perhaps things would have been done differently.[102]

A Flint Seaside Church

In 1849 Pugin had bought land on the opposite side of the road from his house and church perhaps with a view to extending his Catholic community. He even considered linking the two complexes with a bridge inspired, perhaps, by that at Wells, of which he wrote to a friend: 'If you want to be delighted, if you want to be astonished, if you want to be half mad, as I at present am, for God's sake come over to Wells'.[103]

33. 'A vision of 1860': how Pugin thought his land and buildings could later be connected. Letter from Pugin to Hardman (n.d.).

Despatched by Casaretto to 'start a great work',[104] Alcock arrived at Ramsgate on 24 August 1856. Finding St Edward's empty, he reported to Casaretto that 'it was necessary to buy furniture and find a domestic. Mr Luck has kindly offered me a room in his house [The Grange] until things have been arranged'.[105] The monks' efforts to buy the land in 1858 from Mrs Pugin and Edward for £3,000 had to be postponed for lack of funds, despite donations of £1,000 each from Luck and the Digby family. Meanwhile, missions were established at Deal and Gravesend; and after the death of Father Costigan in 1860, the monks took over the mission at Margate. All these centres were very poor, but the work of the monks was supported by their rich patrons in Ramsgate, so that by 1859 the monks had acquired the land and on 21 March 1860 the foundation stone of the monastery was laid. Casaretto's outline plan for an L-shaped building was modified by Luck who donated £4,000 to the project and insisted on a third 'arm', so that the front door was opposite the entrance to the church. In 1861 £200 was paid to Edward Pugin for plans for the monastery, and a further £50 for unexecuted designs. Characteristic details of Edward Pugin are the unusual brick voussoirs round the lancet windows and the heavy weather-boarding round the second-storey dormers.

At the same time, the Pugins expressed a desire to return to The Grange, which may have encouraged Luck to begin building his own home, St Gregory's, behind the monastery. The two storey house with gable ends and a bay window was designed by Edward Pugin. Luck's death in June 1864, leaving St Gregory's to the monastery, strengthened Alcock's determination to open a college, which was realised in 1865. In 1871, Edward designed a three-storey extension to St Gregory's providing a theatre, playroom, study hall and dormitory. The family connection was maintained with Cuthbert Pugin designing fittings for the Tichborne Library in 1888; and Peter Paul Pugin designing not only a further ex-

St Augustine's Church

tension to the College in 1893, but also a new wing for the monastery in 1901 at a cost of £4,000. The foundation was extended again by the building of the Bergh Memorial Library in 1926, while in 1931 the monastery purchased The Grange and St Edwards. Rising numbers necessitated relocating the school to Westgate in 1971, and the subsequent redundancy of St Gregory's resulted in its demolition in 1973.

Although fascinating to ecclesiologists and architectural historians, St Augustine's should not be regarded only as a museum piece, but also as a working church. It is one of the churches of the Catholic Parish of Ramsgate and Minster, and since 2012 has been the official shrine of St Augustine of England, commemorating the coming of the Gospel to this country. Mass is said here daily, offering spiritual succour to all who seek it.

> Let every man build to God according to his means, but not practise showy deceptions; better it is to do a little substantially and consistently with truth.[106]

34. 'I have ... chosen an unobtrusive position behind the figure of Pugin ... the greatest genius in architectural art which our age has produced.' (Sir George Gilbert Scott to General Sir Charles Gray, 1869). Engraving by G.Stodart of part of the frieze by J.B.Philips from the Albert Memorial, designed by Scott.

A Flint Seaside Church

Finally, to conclude this chapter, here is the remarkable illustration drawn by Pugin in 1836, which so well explains and underpins all the architectural beliefs for which he stood.

35. 'They are weighed in the balance and found wanting':
Pugin's opinion of the relative merits of Gothic and Classical architecture (*Contrasts*, 1836)

Other sites of interest 5

This is a select list of buildings, out of a vast number designed by Pugin, chosen to demonstrate their particular relevance to his plans for Ramsgate, together with some typical Kentish churches which may have been a source of inspiration to him.

36. Engraving of Alton Castle, from Ferrey's *Recollections of A.N. Welby Pugin, 1861*

BUILDINGS BY PUGIN

Alton, Staffordshire, Alton Castle (1847) and Hospital of St John the Baptist (1839–52), (RC)

Pugin gained these commissions from the Earl of Shrewsbury. The castle is distinctly Picturesque, perched high above the valley, and complete with battlements and richly coloured roof tiles on the apsidal chapel. The Hospital, separated from the castle by a deep moat, is a harmonious cluster of buildings. An interesting complex which illustrates Pugin's instinctive grasp of medieval form, and can usefully be compared with his plans for Ramsgate.

A Flint Seaside Church

Brewood, Staffordshire, St Mary (1843) (RC)
Pugin designed this unpretentious country church which is situated on the outskirts of the attractive little village of Brewood (pronounced Brood). The exterior clearly reveals the internal plan, and the west tower with broach spire is well proportioned. The adjoining presbytery, schoolhouse and school (with window tracery similar to that in the cloisters of St Augustine's) are built of local red brick with steep roofs, and the plans are asymmetrical. The pared down simplicity of this church, and the sense of community with the adjacent buildings, compare well with St Augustine's.

Cheadle, Staffordshire, St Giles (1841–46) (RC)
Commissioned by the Earl of Shrewsbury, Cheadle, intended to represent an ideal fourteenth-century parish church, is perhaps Pugin's best known work. It is an emphatic and dramatic heavily buttressed red sandstone church, the immensely solid tower with broach spire and crockets rising to a height of 61 metres. The interior is breathtaking. Although every single surface is patterned, it is so well devised that it forms a cohesive whole. It is the antithesis of St Augustine's and serves to illustrate the range of Pugin's work.

37. St Giles' Cheadle: looking towards the high altar

Marlow, Buckinghamshire, St Peter (1845–48) (RC)
Pugin gained this commission from Bloxam's friend Bernard Smith (1815–1903), Fellow of Magdalen College, Oxford, who, under Pugin's influence, converted to Catholicism in 1842. An attractive knapped flint and stone gateway leads to a churchyard and neat grouping of school, master's house and church. The latter is interesting because it was designed at the same time as St Augustine's and is built of similar materials, although the flint is not banded. The church has a single north aisle and is compact and simple. A warning – try to ignore the uncompromisingly modern and angular construction to the east!

Other Sites of Interest

Finally, no description of any of Pugin's work would be complete without referring to:

The Houses of Parliament (1840–52)

Following the fire which destroyed the old Houses of Parliament on 16 October 1834, Pugin was employed as a draughtsman by both Gillespie Graham and Charles Barry, two architects hopeful of winning the competition for the New Palace of Westminster, as it was referred to in those days. Barry, having gained the commission, again had recourse to employ Pugin from August 1836 to January 1837, in the production of detailed drawings for the estimates of cost. It was not until 1844, however, that Pugin became permanently involved in the prestigious project, ostensibly being placed in charge of woodcarving works, but also supplying designs for stained glass, metal work, tiles, wallpapers and upholstery. Hardman, Minton and Crace were called upon to transform Pugin's rapid designs into reality.

If one wishes to see Pugin not only as an architect but also as a polymath – a furniture designer, a brilliant creator of two-dimensional patterns, a decorator who understood the link between interior display and architecture, one has only to step into the House of Lords.

SOME KENTISH CHURCHES

Ash, Kent, St Nicholas (CofE)

A cruciform Early English flint church visited by Pugin. Although heavily restored by Butterfield in 1847, Pugin may still have been influenced by the materials, plan, and typically Kentish tower with external turret, but the real attraction would have been the medieval monumental effigies which form the best collection in Kent. There are also some fine fifteenth and sixteenth-century brasses which would have delighted Pugin. The splendid medieval timber roof in the Molland Chapel was unfortunately not uncovered until 1964, one hundred and twelve years too late for it to gain Pugin's admiration.

Chartham, Kent, St Mary (CofE)

A cruciform thirteenth-century flint church which Pugin would have seen before its sympathetic restoration by G.E.Street in 1873–75. Pugin would have been impressed by the late thirteenth-century timber roofs and the magnificent brass, dated 1306, dedicated to Sir Robert de Septvans. However, the most interesting aspect with relation to St Augustine's is the thirteenth-century grisaille glass with coloured borders set into Kentish tracery. Although Pugin did not follow the split cusp form of tracery, he may have been inspired by the geometrical patterns in the glass together with depictions of clover, hop and passionflower.

A Flint Seaside Church

Herne, Kent, St Martin's (CofE)

An early fourteenth-century flint and ragstone church, visited by Pugin. St Martin's is especially interesting because it has not undergone extensive restoration, and its relevance to St Augustine's can be seen in the countless imaginative gargoyles, both on the exterior and interior. Pugin may have inspected the flint and stone coursing in the lower stage of the tower, and the fifteenth-century brasses. It is also interesting to note that the east ends of the chapels are nearly flush with the east end of the chancel.

38. St Nicholas Church, Ash, from the south: watercolour by Michael Blaker

St Nicholas-at-Wade, Kent, St Nicholas (CofE)

A flint and ragstone thirteenth-century church with remodelling in the following two centuries, close to Ramsgate and visited by Pugin. Like St Martin's, this church has not been restored and can therefore be considered an example of the Thanet churches Pugin hoped to emulate. Indeed, the pointed trefoils in the west window may have been the source for the tracery in the East window of St Augustine's.

Pugin Family Tree

Members of the Family buried in the Pugin Chantry are underlined

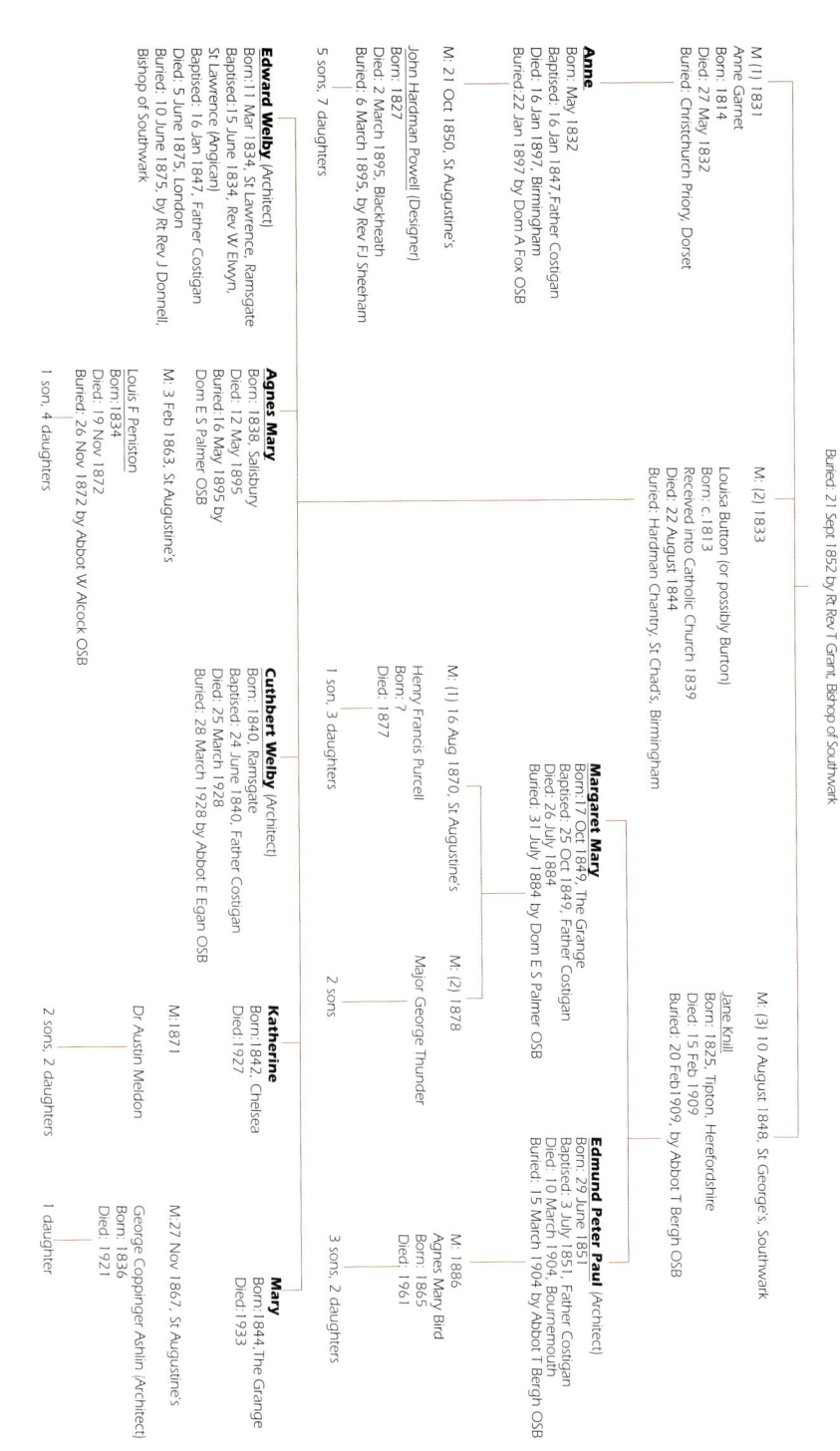

Augustus Charles Pugin (Architect)
Born: c 1769(?)(1769/71), France
Died: 19 Dec 1832, England
Buried: St Mary's, Islington

M: 2 Feb 1802
St Mary's, Islington

Catherine Welby
Born: ?
Died: 28 April 1833
Buried: St Mary's, Islington

M: (1) 1831

Anne Garnet
Born: 1814
Died: 27 May 1832
Buried: Christchurch Priory, Dorset

M: (2) 1833

Augustus Welby Northmore Pugin (Architect)
Born: 1 March 1812, 39 Keppel St, Russell Sq, London
Received into Catholic Church 1835
Died: 14 Sept 1852, The Grange, Ramsgate
Buried: 21 Sept 1852 by Rt Rev T Grant, Bishop of Southwark

Louisa Button (or possibly Burton)
Born: c.1813
Received into Catholic Church 1839
Died: 22 August 1844
Buried: Hardman Chantry, St Chad's, Birmingham

Children of Augustus Welby Northmore Pugin and Anne Garnet:

Anne
Born: May 1832
Baptised: 16 Jan 1847, Father Costigan
Died: 16 Jan 1897, Birmingham
Buried: 22 Jan 1897 by Dom A Fox OSB

M: 21 Oct 1850, St Augustine's

John Hardman Powell (Designer)
Born: 1827
Died: 2 March 1895, Blackheath
Buried: 6 March 1895, by Rev FJ Sheehan

5 sons, 7 daughters

Children of Augustus Welby Northmore Pugin and Louisa Button:

Edward Welby (Architect)
Born: 11 Mar 1834, St Lawrence, Ramsgate
Baptised: 15 June 1834, Rev W Elwyn, St Lawrence (Anglican)
Died: 5 June 1875, London
Buried: 10 June 1875, by Rt Rev J Donnell, Bishop of Southwark

Agnes Mary
Born: 1838, Salisbury
Died: 12 May 1895
Buried: 16 May 1895 by Dom E S Palmer OSB

M: 3 Feb 1863, St Augustine's

Louis F Peniston
Born: 1834
Died: 19 Nov 1872
Buried: 26 Nov 1872 by Abbot W Alcock OSB

1 son, 4 daughters

Cuthbert Welby (Architect)
Born: 1840, Ramsgate
Baptised: 24 June 1840, Father Costigan
Died: 25 March 1928
Buried: 28 March 1928 by Abbot E Egan OSB

Katherine
Born: 1842, Chelsea
Died: 1927

Dr Austin Meldon
M: 1871

Mary
Born: 1844, The Grange
Died: 1933

George Coppinger Ashlin (Architect)
Born: 1836
Died: 1921
M: 27 Nov 1867, St Augustine's

Children of Edward Welby Pugin's branch:

Margaret Mary
Born: 17 Oct 1849, The Grange
Baptised: 25 Oct 1849, Father Costigan
Died: 26 July 1884
Buried: 31 July 1884 by Dom E S Palmer OSB

M: (1) 16 Aug 1870, St Augustine's
Henry Francis Purcell
Born: ?
Died: 1877

1 son, 3 daughters

M: (2) 1878
Major George Thunder

2 sons

Jane Knill
Born: 1825, Tipton, Herefordshire
Died: 15 Feb 1909
Buried: 20 Feb 1909, by Abbot T Bergh OSB

M: (3) 10 August 1848, St George's, Southwark

Edmund Peter Paul (Architect)
Born: 29 June 1851
Baptised: 3 July 1851, Father Costigan
Died: 10 March 1904, Bournemouth
Buried: 15 March 1904 by Abbot T Bergh OSB

M: 1886
Agnes Mary Bird
Born: 1865
Died: 1961

3 sons, 2 daughters

2 sons, 2 daughters

1 daughter

- 53 -

Further reading

A.W.N.Pugin *Contrasts*, Leicester University Press, 1969 (1836), introduction by H.R.Hitchcock
The True Principles of Christian or Pointed Architecture, London: Academy Editions, 1973 (1841)
An Apology for the Revival of Christian Architecture, Oxford: St Barnabas Press, 1969 (1843)
The Present State of Ecclesiastical Architecture in England, Oxford: St Barnabas Press, 1969 (1843)
Floriated Ornament, Shepton Beauchamp: Richard Dennis, 1994 (1849)
A Treatise on Chancel Screens and Rood Lofts, London, 1851

Paul Atterbury and Clive Wainwright (eds), *Pugin, A Gothic Passion*, New Haven and London: Yale University Press, 1994

Margaret Belcher (ed), *The Collected Letters of A.W.N.Pugin*, Vols 1-5, Oxford: Oxford University Press, 2001-15

Michael Fisher, *Alton Towers: A Gothic Wonderland*, Stafford, Fisher, 1999

Pugin-land: A.W.N. Pugin, Lord Shrewsbury and the Gothic Revival in Staffordshire, Stafford: Fisher, 2002

"Gothic For Ever": A.W.N. Pugin, Lord Shrewsbury, and the Rebuilding of Catholic England, Reading: Spire Books, 2012

Rosemary Hill, *Pugin and Ramsgate*, Ramsgate: The Pugin Society, 1999

God's Architect: Pugin and the Building of Romantic Britain, London: Allen Lane, 2007

David Higham and Penelope Carson, *Pugin's Churches of the Second Spring*, Uttoxeter: Hawksworth Graphics & Print Ltd, 1997

Patricia Spencer-Silver, *Pugin's Builder: the Life and Work of George Myers*, Hull: University of Hull Press, 1993; Second edition, Leominster: Gracewing, 2010

Caroline Stanford (ed), *'Dearest Augustus and I': The Journal of Jane Pugin*, Reading, Spire Books, 2004

Phoebe Stanton, *Pugin*, London: Thames and Hudson, 1971

Alexandra Wedgwood, *A.W.N.Pugin and the Pugin Family*, London: Victoria and Albert Museum, 1985

Alexandra Wedgwood (ed), 'Pugin in his home', A Memoir by J.H.Powell, London: Victoria and Albert Museum, 1994 (reprinted from *Architectural History*, Vol 31, 1988)

Notes

1. B.Webb, quoted in J. Mordaunt Crook, 'Benjamin Webb (1819–85) and Victorian Ecclesiology', *Studies in Church History*, 1997, p434
2. Pugin, *Some Remarks on the Articles Which Have Recently Appeared in the 'Rambler', Relative to Ecclesiastical Architecture and Decoration*, London, 1851, p11
3. Letter from Pugin to Bloxam, September 1840, Bloxam Archive, MS 528–8, Magdalen College, Oxford. The emphasis is Pugin's.
4. Letter to Hardman in P.Stanton, *Pugin*, London, 1971, p194
5. Pugin, *True Principles of Christian or Pointed Architecture*, London, 1973 (1841), p76
6. Pugin, *True Principles*, op. cit., p50
7. Pugin, *True Principles*, op. cit., p57
8. Pugin, quoted in P.Stanton, op. cit., p125
9. Pugin, *The Present State of Ecclesiastical Architecture in England*, Oxford, 1969 (1843), p61
10. Pugin, article in the *Dublin Review*, May 1841, quoted in Stanton, op. cit., p125
11. Pugin, *The Present State*, op. cit., p18
12. Pugin, *An Apology for the Revival of Christian Architecture*, Oxford, 1969 (1843), p21
13. Pugin, *Contrasts*, Leicester, 1969 (1836), p6
14. Pugin, *Floriated Ornament*, Somerset, 1994 (1849).
15. Letter from Mrs Pugin, 6 September 1825, Y.747, Yale University Library in C.Wainwright, 'The Antiquary and Collector', P.Atterbury & C.Wainwright, *Pugin, A Gothic Passion*, New Haven and London, 1994, p91
16. Letter from Pugin to Bloxam, c Summer 1845, Bloxam Archive, MS 528–27, Magdalen College, Oxford.
17. Letter from Pugin to Crace, September 1849, PUG 6/11, RIBA in C.Wainwright, 'The Antiquary and Collector', P.Atterbury & C.Wainwright, op. cit., p102
18. (Ed) A.Wedgwood, J.H.Powell, 'Pugin in His Home', London, 1994 (Reprinted from *Architectural History*, Vol 31, 1988), p17
19. J.H.Powell, op. cit., p20
20. Letter from Pugin, n.d., quoted in Dr M.Belcher, typescript notes of a lecture given at Sydney, 1989, Dom Bede Millard OSB files, St Augustine's Abbey, Chilworth, p8
21. Letter from Pugin, n.d., quoted in Dr M.Belcher, op. cit., p8
22. *The Tablet*, 2 January 1847, p5

23	Letter from Pugin, n.d., HLRO/304/518, in R Hill, *Pugin and Ramsgate*, Ramsgate, 1999, p15
24	J.H.Powell, op. cit., p9
25	J.H.Powell, op. cit., p11
26	J.H.Powell, op. cit., p11
27	M.Trappes-Lomax, *Pugin, A Mediaeval Victorian*, London, 1932, p272
28	Pugin, *An Extract from the Popish Creed!*, 1850, SEC 21/4/3, St Edmund's College Archives in Westminster Diocesan Archives.
29	A.Wedgwood, *A.W.N.Pugin and the Pugin Family*, London, 1985, p28
30	Letter to John Hardman, 1847, private collection. We are grateful to Dr M.Belcher for her transcription of this letter.
31	A.Wedgwood, op. cit., p66
32	R.Craig, 'Pugin's Caroline', The Pugin Society, *True Principles*, Vol 1, No 3.
33	Information kindly supplied by Michael Hunt, Ramsgate Maritime Museum.
34	Letter from Pugin to Crace, 2 January 1850, PUG 7/1, RIBA Library.
35	Letter from Pugin to Crace, May 1850, PUG 7/33, RIBA Library.
36	B.Ferrey, *Recollections of A.N.Welby Pugin & his Father Augustus Pugin*, New York, 1972 (1861), p62
37	J.H.Powell, op. cit., p24
38	J.H.Powell, op. cit., p25
39	J.Bossy, *The English Catholic Community 1750–1850*, London, 1975.
40	Letter from Pugin to C.Stanfield, 15 October 1842, SEC 21/4/2/2, St Edmund College Archives in Westminster Diocesan Archives.
41	Pugin, *An Extract from the Popish Creed!*, op. cit.
42	Pugin, 'An Address to the Inhabitants of Ramsgate', *Catholic Magazine and Register*, Vol 12, December 1850, pp328–31
43	E.S.Purcell, *Life of Ambrose Phillipps de Lisle*, II, pp205–6
44	Owen Chadwick, *The Victorian Church, Part 1*, London, 1966, p68
45	Letter from Pugin to Bloxam, May 1841, Bloxam Archive, MS 528–118, Magdalen College, Oxford. We are grateful to Dr M.Belcher for her transcription of this letter.
46	Letter from Pugin to C.Stanfield, n.d., SEC 21/4/2/2, St Edmund College Archives in Westminster Diocesan Archives.
47	J.F.White, *The Cambridge Movement*, Cambridge, 1962, p40
48	Information kindly supplied by Dr R.O'Donnell.
49	Pugin, *The Present State*, op. cit., p51
50	*Ecclesiologist*, New Series, Vol II, 1846, pp10–11
51	Letter from E.Burne-Jones to Mrs Horner (no relation), 1886, in G.Burne-Jones, *Memorials of Edward Burne-Jones*, Vol II, London, 1906, p285
52	Letter from Pugin to 'Rev & Dear Sir' from St Augustine's [The Grange], n.d., PuAW/1/1/1, RIBA Library.
53	Notes with map ref R/U1561 P442(A), Ramsgate Library.
54	*The Builder*, Vol X, No 503, 25 September 1852, p605